How Children Fail REVISED EDITION

DELTA BOOKS OF INTEREST

How Children Fail

REVISED EDITION

JOHN HOLT

With a new introduction by George McGovern

A Merloyd Lawrence Book
DELTA / SEYMOUR LAWRENCE

A MERLOYD LAWRENCE BOOK
A Delta/Seymour Lawrence Edition
Published by
Dell Publishing
a division of
Bantam Doubleday Dell Publishing Group, Inc.
666 Fifth Avenue
New York, New York 10103

Designed by Richard Oriolo

Library of Congress Cataloging in Publication Data

Holt, John Caldwell, 1923–1985
    How children fail.
    "A Merloyd Lawrence book."
    1. Promotion (School)   2. Underachievers.   3. Grade
repetition.   4. Dropouts.   5. Failure (Psychology)
I. Title.
LB3063.H627   1982   371.2′8   81-17335
ISBN: 0-385-28423-3 (pbk.)   AACR2

Manufactured in the United States of America
Previous Delta edition
New Delta edition
November 1988

10   9   8   7   6   5   4

BG

INTRODUCTION
by George McGovern

During the 1960s and 1970s I developed a friendship with the late John Holt based in considerable part on our mutual interest in the education of children. Before entering politics I was a college history teacher, but my interest in education began long before my teaching days.

I have always thought that I was the beneficiary of excellent teachers in the public schools of Mitchell, South Dakota. These teachers—many of them unmarried women whose lives centered on their students and the classroom—were the best. They watched and worried and labored with their students. They were stimulating, imaginative human beings in love with the education and development of the young.

I sensed that John Holt was such a human being—fascinated with young minds and the necessity of opening and challenging those minds to the wonderful world around us. He was convinced that children were "failing" because society—the family, the school, the community—was failing to encourage, to stimulate, to instruct young minds in an intelligent manner.

As a member of Congress especially interested in the issues of education, I exchanged correspondence with John Holt when the first edition of his book *How Children Fail* was shaking the educational world in the mid-1960s. He exerted a strong influence on my thinking about educational matters. Indeed, as a presidential nominee in 1972, I carried John Holt's book in my briefcase on the campaign trail. I knew the book well, and my familiarity with its insights gave me the capacity and confidence to speak forcefully and meaningfully on educational concerns. I remember drawing on John Holt's wisdom in a major campaign speech in New Jersey before a huge convention of the National Education Association.

It is sad to note that children continue to fail in America's schools—perhaps on an even larger scale than when John Holt first wrote of these matters. But a visit to schools in any part of the nation will reveal the same uninspired children and lack of attention to what is being taught of which John Holt wrote a quarter century ago.

It is important to know that the failure of which Holt writes is not limited to a small percentage of students. He believed that most children fail because they are "afraid, bored, and confused." We recognize failure when we see millions of students "dropping out" before they finish high school. But what we do not always see, as John Holt saw, is that most children are failing, in that "they fail to develop more than a tiny part of the tremendous capacity for learning, understanding, and creating with which they were born and of which they made full use during the first two or three years of their lives."

Obviously failure on such a large scale is not to be laid solely at the feet of our teachers. Rather, such a failure embraces the home, the neighborhood, and the whole community. The finest of all teachers are not able to compensate entirely for the failings of home and community.

John Holt argues in this book, reinforcing his argument with many additional insights and experiences in the revised edition, that we must cease coercing children into dull learning exercises without reference to their own personal interests and preferences. The schools at best can cover only a tiny fraction of human knowledge and experience. Thus there is nothing lost and much to be gained in encouraging children to follow their own curiosity about life and to build on thier own personal interests. A boy trying to read a book on science that grips his curiosity should not be scolded and ridiculed by a teacher trying to cram a lesson in history into his head.

The author believes that one of the basic needs of children is to be in the company of adults who are willing and able to listen to the individual child revealing and discussing his or her own concerns, hopes, anxieties, and fears. Too many teachers dislike and distrust children and are themselves fearful of an honest and free-ranging dialogue with their students. Too many teachers are comfortable only with dull and routine ways of conducting their classrooms that ignore the interests and questions of children.

"It is not the subject matter that makes some learning more valuable than others, but the spirit in which the work is done. If a child is doing the kind of learning that most children do in school, when they learn at all—swallowing words, to spit back at the teacher on demand—he is wasting his time, or, rather, we are wasting it for him. This learning will not be permanent or relevant or useful. But a child who is learning naturally, following his curiosity where it leads him, adding to his mental model of reality whatever he needs and can find a place for, and rejecting without fear or guilt what he does not need, is growing in knowledge, in the love of learning, and in the ability to learn."

These convictions of John Holt form the centerpiece of this book and they are worthy of our careful reading and consideration today. It is a measure of the author's boldness and his faith in children that his conclusions after a lifetime of observing and working with students and teachers include this paragraph:

> We cannot have real learning in school if we think it is only our duty and our right to tell children what they must learn. We cannot know, at any moment, what particular bit of knowledge or understanding a child needs most, will most strengthen and best fit his model of reality. Only he can do this. He may not do it very well, but he can do it a hundred times better than we can. The most we can do is try to help, by letting him know roughly what is available and where he can look for it. Choosing what he wants to learn and what he does not is something he must do for himself.

Washington, D.C., 1988

"If we taught children to speak, they'd never learn."
—WILLIAM HULL

"Think things, not words."
—O. W. HOLMES, JR.

ACKNOWLEDGMENTS

Like everyone else, I owe more debts than I can ever repay, or even tell. But to certain people, who have played a particularly important part in the development of this book and the ideas in it, I owe, and give, my special thanks: first, to Robert Cunningham, my English teacher at Exeter, who used to tell us, "Certainty is illusion, and repose is not the destiny of man," and thus, and for the first time, opened my mind to the possibility of doubt and change; then, to John and Anne Holden, directors of the Colorado Rocky Mountain School, and to Mary Wright, headmistress of the Lesley-Ellis School, who gave me classes to teach and left me free to teach them as I thought best, free to make mistakes and to learn what I could from them; to Peggy Hughes, who long urged and finally persuaded me to make these memos into a book; to my sister, Jane Pitcher, from whom I have learned a great deal about little children, and how to live with and enjoy them; to Bill Hull, who, more than anyone, made me look at, see, and think about what was really going on in the classroom and in the minds of the children I was trying to "teach"; finally, and most of all, to the children themselves, who taught me much more than I taught them.

CONTENTS

How Children Fail REVISED EDITION

FOREWORD

Most children in school fail.

For a great many, this failure is avowed and absolute. Close to forty percent of those who begin high school drop out before they finish. For college, the figure is one in three.

Many others fail in fact if not in name. They complete their schooling only because we have agreed to push them up through the grades and out of the schools, whether they know anything or not. There are many more such children than we think. If we "raise our standards" much higher, as some would have us do, we will find out very soon just how many there are. Our classrooms will bulge with kids who can't pass the test to get into the next class.

But there is a more important sense in which almost all children fail: Except for a handful, who may or may not be good students, they fail to develop more than a tiny part of the tremendous capacity for learning, understanding, and creating with which they were born and of which they made full use during the first two or three years of their lives.

Why do they fail?

They fail because they are afraid, bored, and confused.

They are afraid, above all else, of failing, of disappointing or displeasing the many anxious adults around them, whose limitless hopes and expectations for them hang over their heads like a cloud.

They are bored because the things they are given and told to do in school are so trivial, so dull, and make such limited and narrow demands on the wide spectrum of their intelligence, capabilities, and talents.

They are confused because most of the torrent of words that pours over them in school makes little or no sense. It often flatly contradicts other things they have been told, and hardly ever has any relation to what they really know—to the rough model of reality that they carry around in their minds.

How does this mass failure take place? What really goes on in the classroom? What are these children who fail doing? What goes on in their heads? Why don't they make use of more of their capacity?

This book is the rough and partial record of a search for answers to these questions. It began as a series of memos written in the evenings to my colleague and friend Bill Hull, whose fifth-grade class I observed and taught in during the day. Later these memos were sent to other interested teachers and parents. A small number of these memos make up this book. They have not been much rewritten, but they have been edited and rearranged under four major topics: Strategy; Fear and Failure; Real Learning; and How Schools Fail. *Strategy* deals with the ways in which children try to meet, or dodge, the demands that adults make of them in school. *Fear and Failure* deals with the interaction in children of fear and failure, and the effect of this on strategy and learning. *Real Learning* deals with the difference between what children appear to know or are expected to know, and what they really know. *How Schools Fail* analyzes the ways in which schools foster bad strategies, raise children's fears, produce learning which is usually fragmentary, distorted, and short-lived, and generally fail to meet the real needs of children.

These four topics are clearly not exclusive. They tend to overlap and blend into each other. They are, at most, different ways of looking at and thinking about the thinking and behavior of children.

It must be made clear that the book is not about unusually bad schools or backward children. The schools in which the experiences described here took place are private schools of the highest standards and reputation. With very few exceptions, the children whose work is described are well above the average in intelligence and are, to all outward appearances, successful, and on their way to "good" secondary schools and colleges. Friends and colleagues, who understand what I am trying to say about the harmful effect of today's schooling on the character and intellect of children, and who have visited many more schools than I have, tell me that the schools I have not seen are not a bit better than those I have, and very often are worse.

FOREWORD TO REVISED EDITION

After this book came out, people used to say to me, "When are you going to write a book about how *teachers* fail?" My answer was, "But that's what this book is about."

But if it is a book about a teacher who often failed, it is also about a teacher who was not satisfied to fail, not resigned to failure. It was my job and my chosen task to help children learn things, and if they did not learn what I taught them, it was my job and task to try other ways of teaching them until I found ways that worked.

For many years now I've been urging and begging teachers and student teachers to take this attitude toward their work. Most respond by saying, "Why are you blaming us for everything that goes wrong in schools? Why are you trying to make us feel all this guilt?"

But I'm not. I didn't *blame* myself or feel *guilt,* just because my students were so often not learning what I was teaching, because I wasn't doing what I had set out to do and couldn't find out how to do it. But I did hold myself *responsible.*

"Blame" and "guilt" are crybaby words. Let's get them out of our talk about education. Let's use instead the word "responsible." Let's have schools and teachers begin to hold themselves responsible for the results of what they do.

I held myself responsible. If my students weren't learning what I was teaching, it was my job to find out why. *How Children Fail*, as I said, was a partial record of my not very successful attempts to find out why. Now, twenty years after I wrote most of *How Children Fail*, I think I know much more about why. That's what this revised version of the book is about.

I've decided to leave the original exactly as I wrote it, and where I have second thoughts about what I then wrote, I've put those in. It may seem to some that it took me too long to learn what I have learned, and that I made many foolish mistakes, and missed many obvious clues. I feel no guilt about this. I was trying as best I could to discover something difficult and important, and I suspect there was no path to it much quicker or shorter than the one I took. In this book you can see where I began, some of my twistings and turnings, and where I am today.

There is now a lot of talk about raising our standards higher, about "making sure" that children know what they are "supposed to know" before allowing them into the next grade. What will this lead to in practice? Mostly, to a lot more of the fakery I talk about in this book— i.e., giving children intensive coaching just before the tests so that they will appear to know what in fact they do not know at all. Also to a highly selective enforcement of these rules—we can expect to see many more poor and/or non-white children held back than affluent whites. Finally, we will find out once more what by now we should have learned: that many or most children repeating a grade do no better the second time through than they did the first, if even as well. Why should they? If a certain kind of teaching failed to produce learning the first time, why will it suddenly produce it the second time? In many cases the children, now ashamed and angry as well as bored and confused, will do even worse than before—and will probably disrupt the class as well.

In other words, this brave crusade against the evil of "social promotion" is not likely to last long or produce many positive results.

Recently, at a meeting of the Education Writers Association, in New York, I heard Dr. Ronald Edmonds, of the Harvard Graduate School of Education, talk about some important research he had done at the request of the New York City public schools. He and his colleagues tried to find out what makes some schools "effective," by which they meant a school in which the percentage of poor children who learn a satisfactory amount of what they are supposed to learn in any grade, enough to be legitimately promoted, is the same as the proportion of middle-class or affluent children.

The first thing worth noting is that in the entire northeastern section of the United States the researchers were able to find only fifty-five schools that met this very modest definition of "effective."

The researchers then examined these schools to find what qualities they had in common. Of the five they found, two struck me as crucial: (1) if the students did not learn, the schools did not blame *them*, or their families, backgrounds, neighborhoods, attitudes, nervous systems, or whatever. *They did not alibi.* They took full responsibility for the results or nonresults of their work. (2) When something they were doing in the class did not work, they stopped doing it, and tried to do something else. They flunked unsuccessful methods, not the children.

If we could only persuade more teachers and administrators to think this way, we would soon see improvement in our schools. But there seems little chance that this will happen in any near future. All the tendencies point the other way. The worse the results, the more the schools claim that they are doing the right thing and that the bad results are not their fault.

A final observation. The destruction of children's intelligence that I describe here was going on more than twenty years ago.

☐STRATEGY

I can't get Nell out of my mind. When she talked with me about fractions today, it was as if her mind rejected understanding. Isn't this unusual? Kids often resist understanding, make no effort to understand; but they don't often grasp an idea and then throw it away. Do they? But this seemed to be what Nell was doing. Several times she would make a real effort to follow my words, and did follow them, through a number of steps. Then, just as it seemed she was on the point of getting the idea, she would shake her head and say, "I don't get it." Can a child have a vested interest in failure? What on earth could it be? Martha, playing the number game, often acts the same way. She does not understand, does not want to understand, does not listen when you are explaining, and then says, "I'm all mixed up."

There may be a connection here with *producer-thinker* strategies. [We used the word *producer* to describe the student who was only interested in getting right answers, and who made more or less uncritical use of rules and formulae to get them; we called *thinker* the student who tried to think about the meaning, the reality, of whatever it was he was working on.] A student who jumps at the right answer and misses often falls back into defeatism and despair because he doesn't know what else to do. The thinker is more willing to plug on.

It is surprising to hear so many of these kids say "I'm dumb." I thought this kind of thing came later, with the bogey, adolescence. Apparently not.

My room group did fairly well today at the number game. [At certain periods, two thirds of the class was away at art or shop classes, and the rest stayed with me for "room period," a special class, invented by Bill Hull. We met in a small room just off the classroom. There we played various kinds of intellectual games, did puzzles, and held discussions in a way as little like ordinary classroom work as possible. On this occasion we played a game like Twenty Questions, in which the teacher thinks of a number and the students try to find it by asking questions to which the teacher may answer yes or no.] Laura was consistently the poorest asker of questions. It happened that on several occasions her turn came when the choice of numbers had been narrowed down to three or four, and she guessed the number. This made her feel that she was the official number guesser for the day. In one game she made her first guess at an individual number when there were still twelve numbers left to choose from—obviously a poor move. Once she guessed, others started doing the same, and wasted four turns on it. Later on Mary got the idea that she was a mind reader, and started trying to guess the numbers from the beginning. The rest of her team became infected with this strategy for a while, before they went back to the plan of closing in on the number.

On the whole they were poised and collected and worked well as a team, though they didn't eliminate enough numbers at a turn. Thus, knowing that the number was between 250 and 300, they would say, "Is it between 250 and 260?" instead of taking a larger bite.

Nancy played well, but after a point the tension of the game got to be too much for her and her mind just stopped working. She didn't get frantic, like Nell or Martha, or make fantastic guesses; she just couldn't think of anything to say, and so said nothing. A safe policy.

☐ **February 18, 1958**

Intelligence is a mystery. We hear it said that most people never develop more than a very small part of their latent intellectual capacity. Probably not; but *why* not? Most of us have our engines running at about ten percent of their power. Why no more? And how do some people manage to keep revved up to twenty percent or thirty percent of their full power—or even more?

What turns the power off, or keeps it from ever being turned on?

During these past four years at the Colorado Rocky Mountain School my nose has been rubbed in the problem. When I started, I thought that some people were just born smarter than others and that not much could be done about it. This seems to be the official line of most of the psychologists. It isn't hard to believe, if all your contacts with students are in the classroom or the psychological testing room. But if you live at a small school, seeing students in class, in the dorms, in their private lives, at their recreations, sports, and manual work, you can't escape the conclusion that some people are much smarter part of the time than they are at other times. Why? Why should a boy or girl, who under some circumstances is witty, observant, imaginative, analytical, in a word, *intelligent*, come into the classroom and, as if by magic, turn into a complete dolt?

The worst student we had, the worst I have ever encountered, was in his life outside the classroom as mature, intelligent, and interesting a person as anyone at the school. What went wrong? Experts muttered to his parents about brain damage—a handy way to end a mystery that you can't explain otherwise. Somewhere along the line, his intelligence became disconnected from his schooling. Where? Why?

This past year I had some terrible students. I failed more kids, mostly in French and Algebra, than did all the rest of the teachers in the school together. I did my best to get them through, goodness knows. Before every test we had a big cram session of practice work, politely known as "review." When they failed the exam, we had postmortems, then more review, then a makeup test (always easier than the first), which they almost always failed again.

I thought I knew how to deal with the problem: make the work interesting and the classroom a lively and enthusiastic place. It was, too, some of the time at least; many of these failing students actually liked my classes. Overcome children's fear of saying what they don't understand, and keep explaining until they do understand. Keep a steady and resolute pressure on them. These things I did. Result? The good students stayed good, and some may have got better; but the bad students stayed bad, and some of them seemed to get worse. If they were failing in November they were still failing in June. There must be a better answer. Maybe we can prevent kids from becoming chronic failers in the first place.

☐ **February 24, 1958**

Observing in Bill Hull's Class: _____
In today's work period three or four people came up to you for help. All were stuck on that second math problem. None of them had made any effort to listen when you were explaining it at the board. I had been watching George, who had busied himself during the explanation by trying, with a pencil, to ream and countersink a hole in the side of his desk, all the while you were talking. He indignantly denied this. I showed him the hole, which silenced him. Gerald was in dreamland; so for the most part was Nancy, though she made a good recovery when asked a question. Unusual for her. Don listened about half the time, Laura about the same. Martha amused herself by turning her hand into an animal and having it crawl around her desk.

Watching older kids study, or try to study, I saw after a while that they were not sufficiently self-aware to know when their minds had wandered off the subject. When, by speaking his name, I called a daydreamer back to earth, he was always startled, not because he had thought I wouldn't notice that he had stopped studying, but because *he* hadn't noticed.

Except by inflicting real pain on myself, I am never able to stay awake when a certain kind of sleepiness comes over me. The mind plays funny tricks at such times. I remember my own school experience of falling asleep in class while listening to the teacher's voice. I used to find that the "watchman" part of my mind that was saying "Keep awake, you fool!" would wake me when the teacher's voice began to fade. But the part of my mind that wanted or needed sleep was not so easily beaten. It used to (and still does) counterfeit a voice, so that as I fell asleep an imaginary voice continued to sound in my head, long enough to fool me until the watchman no longer had the power to awaken me. The watchman learned, in turn, that this counterfeit voice was liable to be talking about something different, or pure nonsense, and thus learned to recognize it as a counterfeit. Many times, I have dozed off with a voice sounding inside my head, only to have the watchman say "Hey! Wake up! That voice is a phony!"

Most of us have very imperfect control over our attention. Our minds slip away from duty before we realize that they are gone. Part of being a good student is learning to be aware of that state of one's own mind and the degree of one's own understanding. The good student may be one who often says that he does not understand, simply because he keeps a constant check on his understanding. The poor student, who does not, so to speak, watch himself trying to understand, does not know most of the time whether he understands or not. Thus the problem is not to get students to ask us what they don't know; the problem is to make them aware of the difference between what they know and what they don't.

All this makes me think of Herb. I saw the other day why his words so often run off the paper. When he is copying a word, he copies about two letters at a time. I doubt whether he looks beyond them, or that he could tell you, in the middle of a word, what the whole word was. He has no idea, when he begins to copy a word, how long the word is going to be, or how much room it may take up.

☐ **April 21, 1958**

I watched Ruth during the period of the math test. At least four fifths of the time she was looking out the window; or else she played with her pencil, or chewed her fingernails, or looked at Nell to see what information she might pick up. She did not look in the least worried or confused. It looked as if she had decided that math tests were to be done, not during the regular test period, when everyone else does them, but during conference period on Friday, with teacher close at hand, so that if she got into a jam she could get instant help.

She seems to find the situation of not knowing what to do so painful that she prefers to do nothing at all, waiting instead for a time when she can call for help the moment she gets stuck. Even in conference period today she did next to nothing. She was trying to sneak something out of her desk. She moves rather jerkily, so every time she raised the desk lid, I saw it out of the corner of my eye and looked at her. This was rather frustrating for her; however, she kept right on trying for most of the period, not a bit abashed by being caught at it all the time.

Remember when Emily, asked to spell "microscopic," wrote MINCOPERT? That must have been several weeks ago. Today I wrote MINCOPERT on the board. To my great surprise, she recognized it. Some of the kids, watching me write it, said in amazement, "What's that for?" I said, "What do you think?" Emily answered. "It's supposed to be 'microscopic.'" But she gave not the least sign of knowing that she was the person who had written MINCOPERT.

On the diagnostic spelling test, she spelled "tariff" as TEARERFIT. Today I thought I would try her again on it. This time she wrote TEARFIT. What does she do in such cases? Her reading aloud gives a clue. She closes her eyes and makes a dash for it, like someone running past a graveyard on a dark night. No looking back afterward, either.

Reminds me of a fragment of *The Ancient Mariner*—perhaps the world's best short ghost story:

> Like one, that on a lonesome road
> Doth walk in fear and dread,
> And having once turned round walks on,
> And turns no more his head;
> Because he knows, a frightful fiend
> Doth close behind him tread.

Is this the way some of these children make their way through life?

☐ **May 8, 1958**

Memo to the Research Committee: _____

> This school, like many, had a number of academic committees—Math, English, History, etc.—where teachers discussed what they should be teaching. But Bill Hull, who had taught at the school for ten years before I arrived, knew that these committees were not examining children's thinking and work in the way that he and I were trying to do in our class. He thought that some teachers might like to come together from time to time to talk about children's problems with learning, about their intellectual behavior in class, why this behavior so often prevented learning, and what we might do to change that behavior. At the first meeting of this committee, which we called the Research Committee, there were perhaps a dozen teachers. By the second meeting, when it was clearer what Bill wanted to look into and talk about, the number had fallen off. After about three or four meetings there were so few teachers interested in going on with this discussion that we gave up the committee. Nobody seemed to mind.

I have mentioned Emily, who spelled "microscopic" MINCOPERT. She obviously made a wild grab at an answer, and having written it down, never looked at it, never checked to see if it looked right. I see a lot of this one-way, don't-look-back-it's-too-awful strategy among students. Emily in particular has shown instances of it so striking that I would like you to know about them.

Some time after the spelling test in question I wrote MINCOPERT on the blackboard. Emily and one other student—a good speller, interestingly enough—said that it was supposed to be "microscopic." Everyone found this very amusing, including Emily. She is a child who shows in her voice, look, coloring, and gestures much of what she is thinking, and she has not shown the least indication that she knows she is the creator of MINCOPERT. In fact, her attitude suggests that she rejects scornfully the idea that *she* would ever be so foolish as to spell the word in such a way.

Today she handed me, for display, a piece of tagboard on which she had pasted some jokes that a friend had cut out of a newspaper. I found when I got to the last one that she had put the paste on the joke side, so that all there was to read was the meaningless fragment of a news story. I was surprised that she would paste a joke on backwards, without even looking to see whether she had it on the right way. When it was posted, and the other kids were looking at it, I said to Emily, "You'll have to explain that last joke to us; we don't get it." I thought she might look at it, for the first time, see that it was meaningless, and realize that she had pasted it on backside up. To my amazement, she smiled and said with the utmost nonchalance, "As a matter of fact, I don't get it myself." She *had* looked at it. She was perfectly ready to accept the fact that she had posted a joke that was meaningless. The possibility that she had made a mistake, and that the real joke was on the other side, did not occur to her.

I am curious about the ability of children to turn things around in their minds. One day, in room period, I asked the children to write on paper certain words that I had showed them, and then write what these would look like if seen in a mirror. I told them to be sure to write the words exactly as I did, with the same use of capital or lowercase letters. First I wrote CAT. Emily wrote CAt. It didn't trouble her that two letters were capitals and one lowercase—if she noticed it at all. She assumed that seen in a mirror the order of letters would be reversed, so she wrote TaC. The lowercase *t* became capital; the *A* became lower case. The next word was BIRD. She completely forgot what she had just done about reversing the order of the letters. This time she assumed that the trick was to write each letter backwards, while keeping them in the original order. On her paper she had written BIrD. She reversed the *B* correctly, wrote the *I*, then looked at the lowercase *r*, which must have looked to her like an upside-down *L*, decided, "I must turn this right side up," and wrote *L*. Then she decided that the letters *B* and *D* should not be reversed, so her final answer was BILD. Answer to what question? She hadn't the faintest idea. Whatever task she had set out to do at the beginning had gone from her mind long before she got to the end of it; it had become changed into something else, something to do with writing letters upside down, or backwards, or something.

This child *must* be right. She cannot bear to be wrong, or even to imagine that she might be wrong.

When she is wrong, as she often is, the only thing to do is to forget it as quickly as possible. Naturally she will not tell herself that she is wrong; it is bad enough when others tell her. When she is told to do something, she does it quickly and fearfully, hands it to some higher authority, and awaits the magic word *right* or *wrong*. If the word is *right*, she does not have to think about that problem anymore; if the word is *wrong*, she does not want to, cannot bring herself to think about it.

This fear leads her to other strategies, which other children used as well. She knows that in a recitation period the teacher's attention is divided among twenty students. She also knows the teacher's strategy of asking questions of students who seem confused, or not paying attention. She therefore feels safe waving her hand in the air, as if she were bursting to tell the answer, whether she really knows it or not. This is her safe way of telling me that she, at least, knows all about whatever is going on in class. When someone else answers correctly, she nods her head in emphatic agreement. Sometimes she even adds a comment, though her expression and tone of voice show that she feels this is risky. It is also interesting to note that she does not raise her hand unless there are at least half a dozen other hands up.

Sometimes she gets called on. The question arose the other day, "What is half of forty-eight?" Her hand was up; in the tiniest whisper she said, "Twenty-four." I asked her to repeat it. She said, loudly, "I said," then whispered "twenty-four." I asked her to repeat it again, because many couldn't hear her. Her face showing tension, she said, very loudly, "I said that one half of forty-eight is . . ." and then, very softly, "twenty-four." Still, not many of the students heard. She said, indignantly, "Okay, I'll shout." I said that that would be fine. She shouted, in a self-righteous tone, "The question is, what is half of forty-eight. Right?" I agreed. And once again, in a voice scarcely above a whisper, she said, "Twenty-four." I could not convince her that she had shouted the question but not the answer.

Of course, this is a strategy that often pays off. A teacher who asks a question is tuned to the right answer, ready to hear it, eager to hear it, since it will tell him that his teaching is good and that he can go on to the next topic. He will assume that anything that sounds close to the right answer is meant to be the right answer. So, for a student who is not sure of the answer, a mumble may be his best bet. If he's not sure whether something is spelled with an *a* or an *o*, he writes a letter that could be either one of them.

The mumble strategy is particularly effective in language classes. In my French classes, the students used to work it on me, without my knowing what was going on. It is particularly effective with a teacher who is finicky about accents and proud of his own. To get such a teacher to answer his own questions is a cinch. Just make some mumbled, garbled, hideously un-French answer, and the teacher, with a shudder, will give the correct answer in elegant French. The student will have to repeat it after him, but by that time he is out of the worst danger.

Game theorists have a name for the strategy which maximizes your chances of winning and minimizes your losses if you should lose. They call it minimax. Kids are expert at finding such strategies. They can always find ways to hedge, to cover their bets. Not long ago, in room period, we were working with a balance beam. A wooden arm or beam is marked off at regular intervals and balanced on a pivot at its midpoint. The beam can be locked in a balanced position with a peg. We put a weight at a chosen point on one side of the beam, then give the student another weight, perhaps the same, perhaps heavier, perhaps lighter, which he is to place on the other side of the beam so that, when the beam is unlocked, it will stay in the balanced position. When a student has placed the weight, the other members of his group say, in turn, whether they think the beam will balance or not.

One day it was Emily's turn to place the weight. After much thought, she placed it wrongly. One by one, the members of the group said that they thought it would not balance. As each one spoke, she had less and less confidence in her choice. Finally, when they had all spoken and she had to unlock the beam, she looked around and said brightly, "I don't think it's going to balance either, personally." Written words cannot convey the tone of her voice: she had completely dissociated herself from that foolish person (whoever it was) who had placed the weight on such a ridiculous spot. When she pulled the peg and the beam swung wildly, she almost seemed to feel vindicated. Most of the children hedge their bets, but few do it so unashamedly, and some even seem to feel that there is something dishonorable in having so little courage of your own convictions.

I see now that I was wrong about Emily's task. The task for her was not to spell "microscopic," or write a word backwards, or balance a weight. The thought in her mind must have been something like this: "These teachers want me to do something. I haven't got the faintest idea what it is, or why in the world they want me to do it. But I'll do *something,* and then maybe they'll let me alone."

☐ **May 10, 1958**

Children are often quite frank about the strategies they use to get answers out of a teacher. I once observed a class in which the teacher was testing her students on parts of speech. On the blackboard she had three columns, headed Noun, Adjective, and Verb. As she gave each word, she called on a child and asked in which column the word belonged.

Like most teachers, she hadn't thought enough about what she was doing to realize, first, that many of the words given could fit into more than one column and, second, that it is often the way a word is used that determines what part of speech it is.

There was a good deal of the tried-and-true strategy of *guess-and-look,* in which you start to say a word, all the while scrutinizing the teacher's face to see whether you are on the right track or not. With most teachers, no further strategies are needed. This one was more poker-faced than most, so *guess-and-look* wasn't working very well. Still, the percentage of hits was remarkably high, especially since it was clear to me from the way the children were talking and acting that they hadn't a notion of what nouns, adjectives, and verbs were. Finally one child said, "Miss ——, you shouldn't point to the answer each time." The teacher was surprised, and asked what she meant. The child said, "Well, you don't exactly *point*, but you kind of stand next to the answer." This was no clearer, since the teacher had been standing still. But after a while, as the class went on, I thought I saw what the girl meant. Since the teacher wrote each word down in its proper column, she was, in a way, getting herself ready to write, pointing herself at the place where she would soon be writing. From the angle of her body to the blackboard the children picked up a subtle clue to the correct answer.

This was not all. At the end of every third word, her three columns came out even, that is, there were an equal number of nouns, adjectives, and verbs. This meant that when she started off a new row, you had one chance in three of getting the right answer by a blind guess; but for the next word, you had one chance in two, and the last word was a dead giveaway to the lucky student who was asked it. Hardly any missed this opportunity; in fact, they answered so quickly that the teacher (brighter than most) caught on to their system and began keeping her columns uneven, making the strategist's job a bit harder.

In the midst of all this, there came a vivid example of the kind of thing we say in school that makes no sense, that only bewilders and confuses the thoughtful child who tries to make sense out of it.

The teacher, whose specialty, by the way, was English, had told these children that a verb is a word of action—which is not always true. One of the words she asked was "dream." She was thinking of the noun, and apparently did not remember that "dream" can as easily be a verb. One little boy, making a pure guess, said it was a verb. Here the teacher, to be helpful, contributed one of those "explanations" that are so much more hindrance than help. She said, "But a verb has to have action; can you give me a sentence, using 'dream,' that has action?" The child thought a bit, and said, "I had a dream about the Trojan War." Now it's pretty hard to get much more action than that. But the teacher told him he was wrong, and he sat silent, with an utterly baffled and frightened expression on his face. She was so busy thinking about what she wanted him to say, she was so obsessed with that *right answer* hidden in her mind, that she could not think about what he was really saying and thinking, could not see that his reasoning was logical and correct, and that the mistake was not his but hers.

At one of our leading prep schools I saw, the other day, an example of the way in which a teacher may not know what is going on in his own class.

This was a math class. The teacher, an experienced man, was doing the day's assignment on the blackboard. His way of keeping attention was to ask various members of the class, as he did each step, "Is that right?" It was a dull class, and I found it hard to keep my mind on it. It seemed to me that most students in the class had their minds elsewhere, with a mental sentry posted to alert them when their names were called. As each name was called, the boy who was asked if something or other was right answered yes. The class droned on. In time my mind slipped away altogether, I don't know for how long. Suddenly something snapped me to attention. I looked at the teacher. Every boy in the class was looking at him, too. The boy who had been asked if what had just been written was right, was carefully looking at the blackboard. After a moment he said, "No, sir, that isn't right, it ought to be so-and-so." The teacher chuckled appreciatively and said, "You're right, it should be." He made the change, and the class and I settled back into our private thoughts for the rest of the period.

After the boys had left, I thanked the teacher for letting me visit. He said, "You notice I threw them a little curve ball there. I do that every now and then. Keeps them on their toes." I said something in agreement. It didn't seem the time or place to tell him that when he threw his little curve ball the expression in his voice changed enough so that it warned, not only the boys, but also a complete stranger, that something was coming up and that attention had better be paid.

Not long after the book came out I found myself being driven to a meeting by a professor of electrical engineering in the graduate school of MIT. He said that after reading the book he realized that his graduate students were using on him, and had used for the ten years and more he had been teaching there, all the evasive strategies I described in the book—mumble, guess-and-look, take a wild guess and see what happens, get the teacher to answer his own questions, etc.

But as I later realized, these are the games that all humans play when others are sitting in judgment on them.

☐ **July 7, 1958**

I've been reading over the memos from last winter and spring. It is a curious and unsettling process, the business of changing your mind on a subject about which you had very positive convictions. After all I have said and written about the need for keeping children under pressure, I find myself coming to realize that what hampers their thinking, what drives them into these narrow and defensive strategies, is a feeling that they must please the grownups at all costs. The really able thinkers in our class turn out to be, without exception, children who don't feel so strongly the need to please grownups. Some of them are good students, some not so good; but good or not, they don't work to please us, but to please themselves.

Here is Walter, just the opposite, very eager to do whatever people want him to do, and very good at doing it. (By conventional standards he was a very able pupil, so much so that people called him brilliant, which he most assuredly was not.)

We had the problem "If you are traveling at 40 miles per hour, how long will it take you to go 10 miles?"

Walter: 4 minutes.

JH (me): How did you get it?

W: Divided the 40 by the 10.

A quick look at my face told him that this would not do. After a while he wrote, "15 minutes." I wanted to check his understanding.

JH: If you were going 50 miles per hour, how far would you go in 24 minutes?

W (quickly): 36 miles.

JH: How did you get that?

W: Subtracted 24 from 60.

He still hadn't gotten it. I tried again.

JH: If you were going 50 miles per hour, how far would you go in 30 minutes?

W: 25 miles. 30 minutes is half an hour, and half of 50 is 25.

It sounded as if he knew what he was doing at last. I thought he would have no trouble with the 24 minutes problem. But it took a long time, with some hinting from me, before he saw that 24 minutes was 2/5 of an hour, and therefore that he would go 2/5 of 50 miles, or 20 miles, in 24 minutes. Would he have discovered it if I had not paved the way with leading questions? Hard to tell.

Most teachers would have assumed, as I would have once, that when he got the 15-minutes problem, he knew what he was doing. Even the skeptical would have been convinced when he gave his explanation about the 30-minutes problem. Yet in each case he showed that he had not really understood what he was doing, and it is not at all certain that he understands yet.

What was his strategy here? Certainly he was numeral shoving. More than that, he was making up a fairly sensible sounding explanation of how he was doing the problem. And yet, is it not possible, even probable, that in saying that in half an hour you go half of 50 miles, he was merely doing some word shoving to go along with his numeral shoving? The explanation sounded reasonable to me, because, in this case, his way of shoving the numerals happened to be the right way; but he was just as happy with his explanations when he was shoving the numerals the wrong way.

This is a disquieting thought. We say and believe that at this school we teach children to understand the meaning of what they do in math. How? By giving them (and requiring them to give back to us) "explanations" of what they do. But let's take a child's-eye view. Might not a child feel, as Walter obviously did, that in this school you not only have to get the right answer, but you also have to have the right explanation to go with it; the right answer, and the right chatter. Yet we see here that a "successful" student can give the answer and the chatter without understanding at all what he is doing or saying.

Worth noting here that this school, a very selective private school for the high-IQ children of affluent and ambitious parents, despite its radical past and "progressive" reputation had by this time gone Back to the Basics with a vengeance.

☐ **July 25, 1958**

Observing in Bill Hull's Class: _____
Of all I saw and learned this past half year, one thing
stands out. What goes on in class is not what teachers think—certainly not what I had always thought.
For years now I have worked with a picture in mind
of what my class was like. This reality, which I felt I
knew, was partly physical, partly mental or spiritual.
In other words, I thought I knew, in general, what
the students were doing, and also what they were
thinking and feeling. I see now that my picture of
reality was almost wholly false. Why didn't I see this
before?

Sitting at the side of the room, watching these
kids, not so much to check up on them as to find out
what they were like and how they differed from the
teen-agers I have worked with and know, I slowly
became aware of something. You can't find out what
a child does in class by looking at him only when he
is called on. You have to watch him for long stretch-
es of time without his knowing it.

During many of the recitation classes, when the
class supposedly is working as a unit, most of the
children paid very little attention to what was going
on. Those who most needed to pay attention usually
paid the least. The kids who knew the answer to
whatever question you were asking wanted to make
sure that you knew they knew, so their hands were
always waving. Also, knowing the right answer, they
were in a position to enjoy to the full the ridiculous
answers that might be given by their less fortunate
colleagues. But as in all classes, these able students
are a minority. What of the unsuccessful majority?

Their attention depended on what was going on in class. Any raising of the emotional temperature made them prick up their ears. If an argument was going on, or someone was in trouble, or someone was being laughed at for a foolish answer, they took notice. Or if you were explaining to a slow student something so simple that all the rest knew it, they would wave their arms and give agonized, half-suppressed cries of "O-o-o-o-oh! O-o-o-o-oh!" But most of the time, when explaining, questioning, or discussing was going on, the majority of children paid little attention or none at all. Some day-dreamed, and no amount of calling them back to earth with a crash, much as it amused everyone else, could break them of the habit. Others wrote and passed notes, or whispered, or held conversations in sign language, or made doodles or pictures on their papers or desks, or fiddled with objects.

> They went on daydreaming, no matter how often they got caught and embarrassed doing it, because the class, despite our efforts to make it interesting and safe, was a boring, confusing, and dangerous place, from which they would escape if they could—and daydreaming was the only way to escape.

There doesn't seem to be much a teacher can do about this, if he is really teaching and not just keeping everyone quiet and busy. A teacher in class is like a man in the woods at night with a powerful flashlight in his hand. Wherever he turns his light, the creatures on whom it shines are aware of it, and do not behave as they do in the dark. Thus the mere fact of his watching their behavior changes it into something very different. Shine where he will, he can never know very much of the night life of the woods.

So, in class, the teacher can turn the spotlight of his attention now on this child, now on that, now on them all; but the children know when his attention is on them and do not act at all as they do when it is elsewhere. A teacher who is really thinking about what a particular child is doing or asking, or about what he, himself, is trying to explain, will not be able to know what all the rest of the class is doing. And if he does notice that other children are doing what they should not, and tells them to stop, they know they have only to wait until he gets back, as he must, to his real job. Classroom observers don't seem to see much of this. Why not? Some of them do not stay with a class long enough for the children to begin to act naturally in their presence. But even those who are with a class for a long time make the mistake of watching the teacher too much and the children too little. Student teachers in training spend long periods of time in one classroom, but they think they are in there to learn *How To Teach*, to pick up the tricks of child management from watching a *Master At Work*. Their concern is with manipulating and controlling children rather than understanding them. So they watch the teacher, see only what the teacher sees, and thus lose most of what could be a valuable experience.

There should be more situations in which two experienced teachers share the same class, teaching and observing the same group of kids, thinking, and talking to each other, about what they see and hear. Schools can't afford to support this; they can barely pay the one teacher in each class. I should think foundations might be willing to support this kind of work. They seem ready at the drop of a hat to spend millions of dollars on grandiose projects which produce, in the main, only publicity and doctoral dissertations. Perhaps they feel that to have two teachers learn a great deal more about children than they knew before is not worth spending money on. If so, I think they're wrong. When I think what this year's experience has revealed about children's work, behavior, and thought, what avenues of exploration and speculation it has opened up, I can only wonder what extraordinary discoveries about learning might be made if other teachers in other places could work in this way.

This gives a clue about what adults should be doing when they work alone in school classrooms. It is what I came to do more and more in my own fifth-grade class three years later, and what James Herndon describes doing in *How to Survive in Your Native Land.* The teacher first of all tries to prepare a place—a physical, intellectual, and emotional space—in which the students will have a good chance of leading a fairly interesting life. *Then* the teacher's big job is to see what the students do in that space. In G. B. Shaw's *Caesar and Cleopatra,* the queen tells her maids in waiting that Caesar told her to let them say anything they wanted to and that when she asked why she should let them do that, he replied, "So that you can learn from them *what they are.*" Exactly. What we need to learn about our students is what they are, and the way to do this is not to read file folders stuffed full of pseudopsychological diagnoses and long fancy lists of what is wrong with them, but to give them some freedom of thought, speech, and action, as much as the school will allow, and then see what they do.

If we look at children only to see whether they are doing what we want or don't want them to do, we are likely to miss all the things about them that are the most interesting and important. This is one reason why so many classroom teachers, even after years of experience, understand so little about the real nature of children. People teaching their children at home consistently do a good job because they have the time—and the desire—to *know* their children, their interests, the signs by which they show and express their feelings. Only as teachers in schools free themselves from their traditional teacher tasks—boss, cop, judge—will they be able to learn enough about their students to see how best to be of use to them.

When, without any very great plan in mind, I began to allow more and more time during the school day for my students to talk to and do things with each other, I began to learn enough about them, their experiences and ideas and interests, so that I could see some ways to make the classroom a more useful place for them. *They had to teach me before I could begin to teach them.*

Thus when I learned, *from hearing her talk to her friends,* that one of my students loved horses, I was able to help her with her "reading

problem" by putting within her reach a copy of
National Velvet. She loved it, as I thought she
would, and her love for the story and the people
in it gave her the desire and strength to overcome her "reading problem"—which was mostly the fear that she really *couldn't* learn to read,
and the shame she would feel if this proved to
be so.

☐ **July 27, 1958**

It has become clear over the year that these children see school almost entirely in terms of the day-
to-day and hour-to-hour tasks that we impose on
them. This is not at all the way the teacher thinks of
it. The conscientious teacher thinks of himself as
taking his students (at least part way) on a journey to
some glorious destination, well worth the pains of
the trip. If he teaches history, he thinks how interesting, how exciting, how useful it is to know history,
and how fortunate his students will be when they
begin to share his knowledge. If he teaches French,
he thinks of the glories of French literature, or the
beauty of spoken French, or the delights of French
cooking, and how he is helping to make these joys
available to his students. And so for all subjects.

Thus teachers feel, as I once did, that their interests and their students' are fundamentally the same.
I used to feel that I was guiding and helping my
students on a journey that they wanted to take but
could not take without my help. I knew the way
looked hard, but I assumed they could see the goal
almost as clearly as I and that they were almost as

eager to reach it. It seemed very important to give students this feeling of being on a journey to a worthwhile destination. I see now that most of my talk to this end was wasted breath. Maybe *I* thought the students were in my class because they were eager to learn what I was trying to teach, but they knew better. They were in school because they had to be, and in my class either because they had to be or because otherwise they would have had to be in another class, which might be even worse.

Children in school are like children at the doctor's. He can talk himself blue in the face about how much good his medicine is going to do them; all they think of is how much it will hurt or how bad it will taste. Given their own way, they would have none of it.

So the valiant and resolute band of travelers I thought I was leading toward a much-hoped-for destination turned out instead to be more like convicts in a chain gang, forced under threat of punishment to move along a rough path leading nobody knew where and down which they could see hardly more than a few steps ahead. School feels like this to children: it is a place where *they* make you go and where *they* tell you to do things and where *they* try to make your life unpleasant if you don't do them or don't do them right.

For children, the central business of school is not learning, whatever this vague word means; it is getting these daily tasks done, or at least out of the way, with a minimum of effort and unpleasantness. Each task is an end in itself. The children don't care how they dispose of it. If they can get it out of the way by doing it, they will do it; if experience has taught them that this does not work very well, they will turn to other means, illegitimate means, that wholly defeat whatever purpose the task giver may have had in mind.

They are very good at this, at getting other people to do their tasks for them. I remember the day not long ago when Ruth opened my eyes. We had been doing math, and I was pleased with myself because, instead of telling her answers and showing her how to do problems, I was "making her think" by asking her questions. It was slow work. Question after question met only silence. She said nothing, did nothing, just sat and looked at me through those glasses, and waited. Each time, I had to think of a question easier and more pointed than the last, until I finally found one so easy that she would feel safe in answering it. So we inched our way along until suddenly, looking at her as I waited for an answer to a question, I saw with a start that she was not at all puzzled by what I had asked her. In fact, she was not even thinking about it. She was coolly appraising me, weighing my patience, waiting for that next, sure-to-be-easier question. I thought, "I've been had!" The girl had learned how to make me do her work for her, just as she had learned to make all her previous teachers do the same thing. If I wouldn't tell her the answers, very well, she would just let me question her right up to them.

Schools and teachers seem generally to be as blind to children's strategies as I was. Otherwise, they would teach their courses and assign their tasks so that students who really thought about the meaning of the subject would have the best chance of succeeding, while those who tried to do the tasks by illegitimate means, without thinking or understanding, would be foiled. But the reverse seems to be the case. Schools give every encouragement to *producers*, the kids whose idea is to get "right answers" by any and all means. In a system that runs on "right answers," they can hardly help it. And these schools are often very discouraging places for *thinkers*.

Until recently it had not occurred to me that poor students thought differently about their work than good students; I assumed they thought the same way, only less skillfully. Now it begins to look as if the expectation and fear of failure, if strong enough, may lead children to act and think in a special way, to adopt strategies different from those of more confident children. Emily is a good example. She is emotionally as well as intellectually incapable of checking her work, of comparing her ideas against reality, of making any kind of judgment about the value of her thoughts. She makes me think of an animal fleeing danger—go like the wind, don't look back, remember where that danger was, and stay away from it as far as you can. Are there many other children who react to their fears in this way?

☐ **September 22, 1958**

It doesn't take children long to figure out their teachers. Some of these kids already know that what pays off with us is plenty of talk, lots of ideas, even if they are wild. What can we do for the kids who may like to think but don't like to talk?

In my math classes I am on the horns of another dilemma. I want the kids to think about what they are doing. If I make the questions too hard, they begin trying to read my mind, or, as they did this morning, they throw out wild ideas, taking all too literally my statement that a wrong idea is better than none. If, on the other hand, I break the subject down into little lumps, so that when I ask a question most of the class will be able to answer with confidence, am I not doing what I found I was doing for Ruth last year, doing most of their thinking for them?

Perhaps there is no middle position, and what I must do is ask hard questions some of the time, easy questions other times.

The trouble was that I was asking too many questions. In time I learned to shut up and stop asking questions, stop constantly trying to find out how much people understood. We have to let learners decide when they want to ask questions. It often takes them a long time even to find out what questions they want to ask. It is not the teacher's proper task to be constantly testing and checking the understanding of the learner. That's the learner's task, and only the learner can do it. The teacher's job is to answer questions when learners ask them, or to try to help learners understand better when they ask for that help.

We were trying to find out what children understood so that we could help them understand better. But to them our tests of their understanding were just like any other kind of school tests. They just made them more nervous and confused than ever.

□ **October 13, 1958**

What the sixth-grade teachers said the other day suggests that some of our last year's strategists have not reformed. Let's not be too discouraged about this. Given these children whose strategies are shortsighted and self-defeating, these answer grabbers and teacher pleasers, we can to some extent, and over a long period of time, create situations in which some of them may be willing to use their minds in better ways. Some of these, in turn, may even carry these new ways of thinking into a new situation, but we can't expect that they all will. Most of them will probably drop back into the strategies with which they are most familiar and comfortable.

Not many children, in one school year, are going to remake their whole way of dealing with life. With luck, we can give some of them a feeling of what it is like to turn one's full intelligence on a problem, to think creatively, originally, and constructively instead of defensively and evasively. We can hope that they will enjoy the experience enough to want to try it again, but it is only a hope. To put it another way, we can try to give them a glimpse of an intellectual foreign country, and even persuade them to visit it for a while, but it would take more time than we have to make them citizens of that country.

There's no telling what might be done with children if, from their very first days in school, we concentrated on creating the conditions in which intelligence was most likely to grow. Of course, setting up the conditions under which good thinking can be done does not always mean that it will be done.

Take Sam. He seems temperamentally ready to think well, but he rarely does. The other day I had some number series on the board and asked the class to tell me any relationships they could see in them. Sam's first two or three observations were of this order: "There's a one in the top line and a one in the middle line, and there's a two in the third number and a two in the fifth number...." Very trivial, very local, no generality among them at all. Then, in the middle of all this, he came up with a very powerful generalization that I had not even seen myself.

The funny thing is that I don't think he felt that one of these ideas was any better than another. He might one day say that horses and cows were similar in that they were domestic farm animals that ate grass; and the next day that they were alike because he had never ridden on either, or something like that. How can we help him to see that some ways of looking at things, ordering things, are more useful than others?

We have to convince the children that they must not be afraid to ask questions; but further than that, we must get across the idea that some questions are more useful than others, and that to the right kind of question the answer "No" can be as revealing as "Yes." Here is where Twenty Questions, the card game, the balance beam, all come in handy. The scientist who asks a question of nature—i.e., performs an experiment—tries to ask one such that he will gain information whichever way his experiment comes out, and will have an idea of what to do next. He asks his questions with a purpose. This is a subtle art. Can fifth-graders learn some of it?

When Nancy and Sheila worked the balance beam last year, they were often close to the truth, but they could never hang on to it because they could never express their ideas in a form they could test with an experiment. Once one of them said, "Things weigh more further out." This was a big step; but they couldn't think of a way to check or refine this insight, they couldn't ask themselves (to use their terms) how much more things weigh when they get further out.

> The very natural mistake that Bill and I made was to think that the differences between the children in our class had to do with *techniques* of thinking, that the successful kids had good techniques of thinking while the unsuccessful, the "producers," had bad, and therefore that our task was to teach better techniques. But the unsuccessful kids were not trying, however badly, to do the same things as the successful. They were doing something altogether different. They saw the school and their task in it differently. It was a place of danger, and their task was, as far as they could, to stay out of danger. Their business was not learning, but *escaping*.
>
> About three years later I was working, among other things, as a special reading instructor or tutor in the school where for a couple of years I had taught fifth grade. I had persuaded the school to use in its first-grade classrooms Gattegno's *Words in Color,* a very ingenious set of materials, in which each sound of spoken English had its own color.
>
> One of the boys I was tutoring was a seven-

year-old who was not learning to read and was resisting all efforts to teach him. So I was asked to work with him alone. My method was to take letters that I had cut out of one of the *Words in Color* charts, use these letters to make short syllables, and ask him to read them. I see now that it would probably have been better to let him make the syllables and/or words and let me pronounce them—though from time to time we may also have worked in that way.

At any rate, I would use the letters to make a word like PAT. I'd ask him to read it, and he would. Then I would remove the *P* and put a *C* in its place, and ask him to read that. Gattegno called these "transformations," seeing how changing one letter in a word could change the sound of the word—a good idea. The boy would do three or four of these transformations perfectly correctly, though slowly—which meant, I see now, that he really *could* read, really did understand what reading was all about. But then all at once he would spring his nonsense syllable at me. It was always the same one. We might be working with words that had no letter *I* or *T* in them at all—say, RUN, FUN, BUN. Suddenly, when I asked him to read a word, he would say "stut." I would say, "What?" "Stut," he would say, calmly and clearly.

That word rocked me back. Just as I would begin to think "He's really getting it, he's getting the idea of words and sounds," along would come this absurd syllable. How could he have made such a mistake? What did it mean? How was I to deal with it?

It took me a long time—many weeks or even months—to realize that when this boy said "Stut," he was not making a *mistake* at all. He was changing the situation. He had been doing one task that I had given him, to try to figure out the words I had put in front of him. Now he was doing a different task, getting himself a short rest, and me off his back for a while. Indeed, he was giving me a little task of my own, to figure out what in the world made him say "stut," and what in the world I was going to do about it. The ball had been in his court; now it was in mine.

Eventually I figured out what was happening. Perhaps it was the way he was looking at me— not at all the rather tense and concentrated way he looked at the words, but calmly and curiously. He was looking to see what I would do next. I was now his guinea pig, not he mine.

Since by this time I already knew the strategy of guess-and-look, I had learned, when I gave him a word to decode, to turn away so that he could not see my face. If he made a wrong guess or choice, I simply sat there and waited for him to make another. I said nothing; I let him be in charge of the pace of our work. But when he said "stut," I usually turned round to look at him. In time I learned not to do that. When he said "stut," I said nothing, did not move, just waited. Often there might be a silence of a minute or two. Then the boy, having meanwhile had a nice rest, would realize that somehow the ball had got out of my court and back into his. After a while he would go on with his work.

None of this accomplished much, for reasons not clear to me then but much clearer now. This boy could in fact read, could "decode" simple words. But he did not want to, and had decided to refuse to.

It would probably have been much more useful for him and for me if I had used our time together to read aloud to him from books of his choosing, or let him read them silently, with the understanding that whenever he wanted, he could ask me what a word meant and I would tell him—without any questions, explanations, or sound-it-outs.

☐ **December 7, 1958**

Some of our strategists at work:

Atlas Paper #2 asks the students, "What two key words on each index page of the Atlas tell at a glance which names can be found on that page?" The students are supposed to notice that the first and the last place names on any page are printed in larger type at the top of the page—as in a dictionary. The other day, Abby and Jane could not understand what the instructions were asking them to do, largely because they were too busy thinking about the answer to be able to think about the instructions. We studied the examples given in the paper, but to no avail. Finally I told them to sit at their desks and think about it some more. A minute or two later Jane appeared at the door and said indignantly, "Are you *sure* that it isn't those two words at the top of the page?" Having said no such thing, I was taken aback, and said with some surprise, "When did I say that?" She immediately turned to Abby, who was waiting outside the door, and said, "Write it down!" She had all the clues she needed.

☐ March 21, 1959

Here are some of the children working on the balance beam experiment (described in the memo of May 8, 1958). One child has placed the weight where he thinks it will balance the beam; the others are being asked to predict whether it will balance.

Abby: It might move a little to one side—not much.

Elaine: It might teeter a little, then balance, but not really. (She really is covering all the possibilities.)

Rachel: It might balance.

Pat: It will balance pretty much.

Elaine: Teeter totter a teeny bit, then balance.

In this next example, $4 \times 5''$ means that we put four weights five inches out on the beam. $2 \times ?$ means that we gave the child 2 weights to place. In this case, $2 \times 10''$ would have made the beam balance.

$4 \times 5''$; $2 \times ?$ Elaine put them at $2''$, then at $1''$, then at $9''$. I asked, "Is that your choice?" She said, "Yes, but I don't think it will balance." The object of the experiment was to make it balance! She decided to leave the weights at $9''$.

Asked if it would balance, Hester said, "Somehow I think it might."

$8 \times 2''$; $4 \times$?

Rachel (moving the weights back and forth without conviction): Probably won't balance.

Barbara: Put them where you think it *will*. (Barbara is one of our few positive strategists, and so in everything she does.)

Rachel put the weights at 1". Needless to say, the beam did not balance.

$3 \times 2''$; $6 \times$? Hester scattered the six blocks all over the beam, as if in the hope that one of them might hit the magic spot.

Barbara's turn. Everyone will predict that the beam will balance.

$2 \times 3''$; $1 \times$? First she put them at 5". She is counting out lines instead of spaces. Then she saw her mistake, and put them at 6". Everyone except Hester said yes, the beam would balance.

$1 \times 10''$; $2 \times$?

Barbara: $2 \times 5''$. Then she said confidently but with some excitement in her voice, "It's going to do it!"

Elaine: You put a block here (1"), it makes it lighter; here (5") makes it heavier.

When his turn came, Garry said, "I think it's just going to go down—that's safer."

$1 \times 10''$; $1 \times$? Betty put the weight at 10".

Gil: May go down a little and then come back up.

Garry: It will be about even.

Betty: I sort of think it's going to balance.

$4 \times 6''$; $4 \times$? Ralph put them at 6". But two members of the group predicted that it would not balance; then Betty spoke up: "I'll say it will, just in case it does, so we won't get too low a score." Talk about minimax!

Our way of scoring was to give the groups a point for each correct prediction. Before long they were thinking more of ways to get a good score than of making the beam balance. We wanted them to figure out how to balance the beam, and introduced the scoring as a matter of motivation. But they outsmarted us, and figured out ways to get a good score that had nothing to do with whether the beam balanced or not.

$4 \times 9''$; $4 \times$? Sam put them at $9''$. Ralph said, "He didn't trust me, but I'm going to trust him, because that's where I would have put it."

Later, Sam said to another player, "Do what you think is right." To which Betty, usually a positive character, said, "Play safe."

At about this point Betty figured out that the way to get a good score was to put the weights in what you know is a wrong place, and then have everyone on your team say that it is wrong. Thus they will each get a point for predicting correctly. Later, Nat said, "Are *no* votes just as good as *yes* votes?" It was a good question; we should have made *yes* votes count much more.

Another group working.

$4 \times 8''$; $4 \times$? Tony put them at $7''$, then said, "Get ready to disagree." Then he changed them to $8''$. All predicted *yes,* but Nat hedged.

Later, when it was his turn to predict, Nat said, "Too bad you have to be so specific."

Worth noting here that a couple of years later, when I put a balance beam and some weights on a table at the back of my class, and just left it there without saying anything about it or trying to "teach" it, most of the children in the class, including some very poor students, figured out just by messing around with it how it worked.

☐ April 28, 1959

Here are some notes from the other day, when the fourth-graders were playing Twenty Questions.

Many of them are very anxious when their turn comes to ask a question. We ask them to play Twenty Questions in the hope that, wanting to find the hidden thought, they will learn to ask more informative and useful questions.

They see the game quite differently: "When my turn comes, I have to ask a question." They are not the least interested in the object of the game, or whether their question gains useful information. The problem is simply to think of a question, any old question. The first danger is that you will just be sitting there, unable to think of a question. The next danger is that when you ask a question, other kids will think it is silly, laugh at it, say "That's no good."

So the problem becomes not just thinking up a question, but thinking up a question that will sound good. The best way to do this is to listen to kids that you know are pretty sharp, and ask questions that sound like theirs. Thus, a child who found in one game that "Is it water?" was a useful question, went on asking it in game after game, even when other questions had established that the information sought for had nothing to do with water.

Many of our kids play the same way. Pat, Rachel, and some others never have any idea what the object of the game is, or what information has been gained by questions already asked. All they want, when their turn comes, is to have a question that won't be laughed at. Jessie plays it even safer than that. She just refuses to ask a question, says, "I pass," and looks very pleased with herself after she says it, too.

> A man wrote us a letter at Growing Without Schooling telling about the spelling strategy he used at school. When asked to spell a word that he was not one hundred percent sure of, he simply stood up—and said nothing. No guesses, no questions—just dead silence. The children, who would almost certainly have laughed at his wrong guesses, admired his silence. Apparently he didn't get into any trouble over this, since his teachers did not interpret his silence as defiance. It was a perfect school strategy.
>
> Bill and I had our silent strategists. They clearly understood that in keeping quiet they were not doing what we wanted, but they still thought it was their best bet.

Another popular strategy is the disguised blind guess. When kids first play this game, every question is a guess. Then some of them see that it is silly to guess right at the beginning, and that the sensible thing to do is narrow down the possibilities. They criticize very severely teammates who start guessing too soon. So the trick becomes to ask a guessing question that doesn't sound like a guess, like Nat's classic, "Was he killed by Brutus?" This has become something of a joke in his group. Still, every question he asks conceals a guess.

One day we were using the atlas, and the field of the game was geographical locations. Sam wanted to ask if it was Italy, but that was a guess, so he said, "Does it look like a boot?" Every time it is his turn, he says, "Can I make a guess?" The strategy of narrowing down possibilities has not occurred to him, or if it has, he does not know how to make use of it.

Betty makes multiple guesses. Thinking of either Corsica or Sardinia, she asked, "Does it begin with C or S?" Another time she said, "Does it begin with B, D, C, P, or T?" This is not bad strategy. On another occasion she said to a cautious teammate, "Don't say 'Could it be?'; say 'Is it?'" She's a positive little critter.

Sometimes we try to track down a number with Twenty Questions. One day I said I was thinking of a number between 1 and 10,000. Children who use a good narrowing-down strategy to find a number between 1 and 100, or 1 and 500, go all to pieces when the number is between 1 and 10,000. Many start guessing from the very beginning. Even when I say that the number is very large, they will try things like 65, 113, 92. Other kids will narrow down until they find that the number is in the 8,000's; then they start guessing, as if there were now so few numbers to choose from that guessing became worthwhile. Their confidence in these shots in the dark is astonishing. They say, "We've got it this time!" They are always incredulous when they find they have not got it.

They still cling stubbornly to the idea that the

only good answer is a *yes* answer. This, of course, is the result of the miseducation in which "right answers" are the only ones that pay off. They have not learned how to learn from a mistake, or even that learning from mistakes is possible. If they say, "Is the number between 5,000 and 10,000?" and I say yes, they cheer; if I say no, they groan, even though they get exactly the same amount of information in either case. The more anxious ones will, over and over again, ask questions that have already been answered, just for the satisfaction of hearing a *yes*. Their more sophisticated teammates point out in vain that it is silly to ask a question when you already know the answer.

There is a very simple question that hardly anyone seems to have asked. Of the things we teachers do, which help learning and which prevent it? The reason we so seldom ask the question is that we tend to assume that unless there's something wrong with the student, *all* teaching produces learning, so that all we need to think about is what children should be made to learn.

Once we understand that some of the things we teachers do may be helpful, some merely useless, and some downright harmful, we can begin to ask which is which. But only *teachers* can ask such questions and use their daily work with students to test their answers. All other kinds of research into ways of improving teaching lead mostly to expensive fads and nonsense.

With the possible exception of economics, education is probably the largest field of human activity in which there is almost no connection between theory and experience, in which people rarely *test* theories to see if they work and reject or change them if they don't.

Bill Hull and I, in our early work together in the fifth grade, saw correctly enough that the reason so many children in our classes learned so little was that they used such bad thinking and problem-solving strategies. What I did not see until later was that *we*, our classroom, our position as teachers, which is to say, givers of orders, judges, graders, were the *source* of these children's strategies. *We*, and not math, or reading, or spelling, or history, were the problem that the children had designed their strategies to cope with.

It was only later, in another school, that I began to wonder, more intuitively than consciously, how I might help make a class in which children, free of danger from me *and each other*, might once again, as when they were little, reach out hungrily to reality. This is the most important task of a teacher, certainly of younger children—to make or make accessible a part of the world or of human experience which is as interesting, exciting, meaningful, transparent, and emotionally safe as possible.

This is of course what most people do who "teach" their children at home, and how they do it is described in great detail in my book *Teach Your Own*. But teachers still working in classrooms could learn many useful things from these parents' accounts of their own work.

☐FEAR & FAILURE

When I wrote earlier of making the children safe from each other I was not thinking so much of physical violence (though that is everywhere a problem, even in the earliest grades) as of spiritual violence. Hundreds of people—teachers, former teachers, student teachers, parents teaching their own children, children themselves—have told me that in the classrooms they have seen, children who can't do things or do them wrong are made fun of by the other children *and very often by the teachers themselves.* Most children in school are at least as afraid of the mockery and contempt of their peer group as they are of the teacher.

When I began to teach my own fifth-grade class I decided to try to change that, not so much because I had some big theory about how this would affect learning—the theories came later—as because I generally like children and enjoy their company, and I hate to see them behaving meanly and cruelly.

Many of my students came to me from a fourth-grade class in which the teacher, in many ways intelligent and kindly, had (like many teachers) a strong need to feel herself the only source of authority and security in the room. She was not mean to children, and many of the children in her class liked her. But it had apparently never occurred to her to try to prevent the children from being mean to each other—except, of course, when this took such noisy or violent forms that it disrupted the class. In the first place she would probably have said, "What difference does it make whether the children are mean to each other, why should I work on that problem when I have so many others?"

In the second place she probably thought, like most adults, that children are "naturally" cruel and that there was nothing she could do about that, except perhaps to set some outside limits on their cruelty. Or perhaps, looking at the children only to see whether they were being good (doing what she wanted) or bad (not doing it), she did not even notice what they were doing to each other. Only a year ago a friend of mine told me that in one of the "best" schools in this area the ten-year-old daughter of a friend of hers had been made the miserably unhappy victim of a nobody-talk-to-her conspiracy by the other children, *which had gone on for many weeks without their teacher even noticing it.*

Well, these are all afterthoughts. What I noticed at the time, when the school year began, was that the children, eager to put themselves one up with me and their classmates one down, were great tattletales, always running up to me saying, "Mr. Holt, so-and-so said or did such-and-such." I hated this, couldn't stand it. So when children ran up with these stories I would look them in the eye and say in a kind but firm voice, "Mind your own business." They were astonished. Their mouths fell open. I often had to say it twice: "Mind your own business." I might then add something like this: "Thank you for telling me, I appreciate your wanting to help, but (pointing to eyes) I can see, (and to ears) I can hear, and just with what I can see and hear I have plenty to keep me occupied. So unless someone is really hurt or in physical danger, hanging out the window holding on by three fingers (we were on the third floor), I don't want to hear about it." The children would walk away puzzled. What kind of class was this? But they learned the lesson quite fast—it didn't take more than a few weeks for the tattling to stop.

Let me emphasize again that I did not then have a theory in mind that if I could make a cooperative class the children would learn a great deal from each other. If someone had suggested this to me, I might even have been skeptical. No, I simply wanted to stop, as far as I could, the pettiness, meanness, and cruelty, just because it spoiled my pleasure in the classroom and my work. Given that much of a signal from me, the children were happy to stop. *They* then created the cooperative class, and *they* then taught me how much in such a class they could help and teach and learn from each other. My part in this was that I allowed it to happen, allowed space and time for it to happen, and saw, and was pleased, and let the children see I was pleased, that it was happening.

All of this is something that schools and/or teachers could easily do. It costs no more money than what they are already doing. The only problem is that teachers who try to do this, in schools where it has not been made school policy, may get in trouble—as I got in trouble, as Jim Herndon (see *The Way It Spozed to Be*) got in trouble, as any and all teachers get in trouble whose ideas of order are different from the schools'.

Ideas of order. The phrase comes from a poem by Wallace Stevens—"Ideas of Order at Key West."

To give a better glimpse of some of my ideas of order, let me tell about the Q.

In the first school, where I worked with Bill Hull, Bill left me more and more in charge of the class, since he was often busy doing math research with one or two teachers in the early grades. By the late winter and spring of my second year at that school, it had become almost more my class than his. I could tolerate and indeed liked a somewhat higher level of noise and activity in the class than he did, and so allowed it. But this posed me a problem. I wanted to give children plenty of chance to talk to each other and enjoy each other's company. But children are energetic and excitable and tend to get carried away. I needed a way to control the noise, and cut it out altogether if I had to. I didn't want a permanently quiet classroom, but neither did I want to get into the business of telling the children—i.e., yelling at them—to be quiet.

So I invented the Q. I explained to the class why I thought I needed this invention, said that I liked to give them plenty of chances to talk, but that sometimes the talk grew too loud, and sometimes I needed quiet so that I could tell or explain something. So when I wanted quiet I would write a capital Q in a corner of the blackboard. When it was up, the standard school rule went into effect: no talking unless you raise your hand and get permission. On a big piece of cardboard I wrote down the rule: "When the Q is on the board, there shall be no talking except by those who have raised their hand and had permission." That was the Q sentence. If children talked when the Q was on the board, I put a mark opposite their names; this was. called, "Giving them a Q." The penalty was that when recess came, for every Q you had you had to write down the Q sentence once before you could go off and play. Three Q's, three sentences.

Later I made the sentence a bit shorter, as I didn't want to use up too much of the children's recess time, partly because I thought it was very important to them, and partly because the true value of the Q penalty was its nuisance value, in having to do it at all, in having to spend time, if only a minute, writing down some fool sentence when everyone else was rushing out into the play yard and getting things organized. A minute of this writing was just as effective a deterrent as five minutes would have been, maybe more so.

So that was the Q. When I first put the Q on the board, in the corner, I drew a little box around it (see illustration). Children being great lawyers, they began to argue that the Q was not *officially* on the board until the box had been drawn. I agreed to that. And then, slowly, the children invented or developed a delightful custom. When I began to write the Q they would all make some kind of hum or murmur or sound, which would get louder and louder, rising to a shriek as I boxed in the Q with a flourish. But as soon as my chalk hit the edge of the blackboard, completing the box, dead silence.

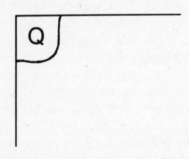

Now and then I wondered, as we grew used to the Q, whether I ought to take some steps about that pre-Q shriek. But I didn't. In the first place, I loved it; it said and says so much about the exuberance and inventiveness of children, how they can make something interesting out of the simplest materials, out of next to nothing, even out of something they don't really like. In the second place, I realized, at first intuitively, later with much thought, that the shriek was part of what made the Q work—and it worked very well. It was the children's way of making that Q theirs as well as mine, and because it *was* theirs as well as mine, they respected it.

Later, realizing that much of the time what I wanted was quiet, not silence, I modified the Q. When I wrote a lowercase q in the corner of the board, it meant that whispering was okay; for talking out loud, the regular Q rule still applied.

A year later, when I had my own fifth-grade class in another school, I reintroduced the Q. I told the children that I had invented the Q in my previous class, explained why I had invented it, and said that it had worked. I told them nothing else about it. But within a week or two of my introducing the Q, this class reinvented the shriek. At first the children simply talked louder and louder as they saw me putting the Q up, but soon the system was exactly the same, at first a hum and murmur as they saw me start writing—and I wrote the Q as fast as I could— rising to a shriek at the end, which was abruptly cut off when my chalk completed the box around the Q.

I was more surprised and delighted than I can say when this happened. Now, I feel quite sure that in any classes where children feel safe and at home, if teachers introduce the Q, the children will soon invent the Q shriek. I hope teachers are wise enough to let them.

Only once, in that later class, did the children test the Q. The class was by this time far more informal than the class in the earlier school, and much more at ease with me. One day when the Q was up, some of the bolder students, including some of my special favorites, began to talk a lot. I began frantically writing down marks. Other children saw what was happening, and began to talk as well. Mutiny! The game began to be, see how fast we can make Mr. Holt write down marks. After a while I saw clearly what was happening. I stopped everything and gave the class a little speech, about like this: "Look, everyone, I know what's happening here. You're trying to find out whether you can wreck the Q system, and the answer is, of course you can. It only works because basically you think it's a pretty fair and sensible system and are willing to let it work. The only thing is, if we lose the Q system, what are we going to put in its place? I have to have *some* way of getting quiet, or silence, in this room if I feel I need it. I like to let you guys talk, even if it gets fairly noisy at times, but I have to be able to control it. If I don't have the Q, I'll have to control it the way the other teachers try to, which is not to let you talk at all." I went on to ask if they thought the Q system was unfair. Nobody did. I asked if they wanted to change it in some way. Nobody did. I said, "Well, okay, let's start again. You've proved your point, the system can't work unless you want it to work. Now I'll throw out this sheet of Q marks and we'll go back to the old system." Which we did. They never tested the Q again. And I have to say that as the year went on and the class became more and more everyone's class, and not just mine, the children became good enough at controlling their own noise so that I had less and less need for the Q. Indeed, if I put it up, it was usually because the children themselves, wanting a little more peace and quiet, would ask me to.

But the ideas of order of all too many schools are that order should, must, can only rest on fear, threat, punishment. They would rather have systems of order based on fear, *even when they don't work,* than systems of order based on the children's cooperation—that work.

☐ **March 27, 1958**

We agree that all children need to succeed; but do we mean the same thing? My own feeling is that success should not be quick or easy, and should not come all the time. Success implies overcoming an obstacle, including, perhaps, the thought in our minds that we might not succeed. It is turning "I can't" into "I can, and I did."

We ought also to learn, beginning early, that we don't always succeed. A good batting average in baseball is .300; a good batting average in life is a great deal lower than that. Life holds many more defeats than victories for all of us. Shouldn't we get used to this early? We should learn, too, to aim higher than we think we can hit. "A man's reach should exceed his grasp, or what's a Heaven for?" What we fail to do today, we, or someone, may do tomorrow. Our failure may pave the way for someone else's success.

Of course we should protect a child, if we can, from a diet of unbroken failure. More to the point, perhaps, we should see that failure is honorable and constructive, rather than humiliating. Perhaps we need a semantic distinction here, between nonsuccess and failure.

It is tempting to think that we can arrange the work of unsuccessful students so that they think they are succeeding most of the time. But how can we keep secret from a child what other children of his own age, in his own or other schools, are doing? What some of these kids need is the experience of doing something really well—so well that they know themselves, without having to be told, that they have done it well. Maybe this means that someone must supply them, from outside, with the concentration and resolution they lack.

I wrote this memo quite early in my collaboration with Bill, when I was still wearing, like an old torn shirt, shreds of my old conventional teacher's notion that somehow we could make children do this or that by "holding them up to high standards."

What I was talking about when I wrote this memo was the idea, common in many schools, the idea behind programmed instruction, that the way to make children feel good about themselves is to give them things to do that are so easy that they can't help but do them. It rarely works. If we and not the children choose the task, then they think about us instead of the task, with the crippling results I have shown. We can then only guarantee success by making the task so incredibly easy that the children cannot find any pleasure or pride in doing it.

The point I now want to make is that "success," as much as "failure," are adult ideas which we impose on children. The two ideas go together, are opposite sides of the same coin. It is nonsense to think that we can give children a love of "succeeding" without at the same time giving them an equal dread of "failing."

Babies learning to walk, and falling down as they try, or healthy six- and seven-year-olds learning to ride a bike, and falling off, do not think, each time they fall, "I failed again." Healthy babies or children, tackling difficult projects of their own choosing, think only when they fall down or off, "Oops, not yet, try again." Nor do they think, when finally they begin to walk or ride, "Oh, boy, I'm succeeding!" They think, "Now I'm walking! Now I'm riding!" The joy is in the act itself, the walking or the riding, not in some idea of success.

Actually, even for adults, "succeed" (if we are not using it to mean getting rich and famous) only applies to two-valued tasks like solving a puzzle or winning a contest, where you have clearly either done it or not done it. This has nothing to do with most tasks and skills that we do all the time, all our lives, and get better at as we do them. Playing the cello, learning a new and (for me) difficult piece, like the string quartets I am working on—Dvorak's "American" and Schubert's "Death and the Maiden"—I may set myself a short and specific task, like learning to play certain sections from memory or to play a certain passage at a certain metronome speed. Of such tasks I can sometimes say "Now I have succeeded." (Though I may have to do the task again a day or two later.) But it is meaningless to talk of "succeeding" in playing the cello, or even in playing these quartets. There is no line with *Success* written on one side and *Failure* on the other. These words seriously distort our understanding of how we, as well as children, do things and do them better.

Children who undertake to do things, like my five-year-old friend Vita who is beginning the very serious study of the violin, do not think in terms of success and failure but of effort and adventure. It is only when pleasing adults becomes important that the sharp line between success and failure appears.

☐ **December 3, 1958**

The other day I decided to talk to the other section about what happens when you don't understand what is going on. We had been chatting about something or other, and everyone seemed in a relaxed frame of mind, so I said, "You know, there's something I'm curious about, and I wonder if you'd tell me." They said, "What?" I said, "What do you think, what goes through your mind, when the teacher asks you a question and you don't know the answer?"

It was a bombshell. Instantly a paralyzed silence fell on the room. Everyone stared at me with what I have learned to recognize as a tense expression. For a long time there wasn't a sound. Finally Ben, who is bolder than most, broke the tension, and also answered my question, by saying in a loud voice, "Gulp!"

He spoke for everyone. They all began to clamor, and all said the same thing, that when the teacher asked them a question and they didn't know the answer they were scared half to death. I was flabbergasted—to find this in a school which people think of as progressive; which does its best not to put pressure on little children; which does not give marks in the lower grades; which tries to keep children from feeling that they're in some kind of race.

I asked them why they felt gulpish. They said they were afraid of failing, afraid of being kept back, afraid of being called stupid, afraid of feeling themselves stupid. Stupid. Why is it such a deadly insult to these children, almost the worst thing they can think of to call each other? Where do they learn this?

Even in the kindest and gentlest of schools, children are afraid, many of them a great deal of the time, some of them almost all the time. This is a hard fact of life to deal with. What can we do about it?

☐ **December 30, 1958**

All fall long, I wondered why Jack fell down so much playing soccer. He is an agile, well-coordinated boy. His balance is good. People don't knock him over. Why was he on the ground so often? Suddenly, the other day, I had the answer.

I discovered it while trying to learn to control the tension that builds up in me when I practice the flute. Music is a good thing for teachers to study, because it creates in us the kind of tension that children live under all the time in the classroom, and that most adults have long forgotten. Incidentally, it is most interesting when Gattegno explains the Cuisenaire rods[1] to teachers, to see them under this very tension. They react to it very much like children, by getting sore at Gattegno, or fighting his ideas, by saying in elaborate language what fifth-graders say when they are startled by a new idea— "This is crazy, nutty, cuckoo."

I have observed many times that children who can do one or two problems of a certain kind, with no trouble, collapse when given a big sheet of them. Something like this is true of exercises in music. When I am trying to play an exercise at (for me) high speed, I am under tension. If the exercise is short, I feel that I can get through it before tension gets the better of me. But if it is long, I am less confident from the start that I can get through without a mistake, and as I play, the inner voice that comments on what I am doing says: "All right so far;

[1]See footnote, p. 138.

watch that G sharp; oops! narrow escape, you almost played F sharp instead of F natural, etc., etc." The voice gets louder and louder, until finally the communication channels are clogged up, coordination breaks down, and I make the mistake I have been fearing to make.

I haven't forgotten Jack and his falling down. One thing I have discovered is that there is a peculiar kind of relief, a lessening of tension, when you make a mistake. For when you make one, you no longer have to worry about whether you are going to make one. Walking a tightrope, you worry about falling off; once fallen off, you don't have to worry. Children, for whom making mistakes is acutely painful, are therefore under great tension when doing something correctly. Worrying about the mistakes they might make is as bad as—no, worse than—worrying about the mistakes they have made. Thus, when you tell a child that he has done a problem wrong, you often hear a sigh of relief. He says, "I *knew* it would be wrong." He would rather *be* wrong, and know it, than not know whether he was wrong or not.

Well, the reason Jack falls down is that this relieves him, for a few seconds, of the great tension he is under when he plays soccer. Being small, he is afraid of crashing into bigger boys, but he is also afraid of showing his fear, and resolutely tries to play the game as he feels he should. This puts his nervous system under a strain that is too much for it. Being a boy, he can't pull out of the game, as a girl might do, or just get out of the way of bigger boys when they come at him. So every now and then he falls down, and thus gets an honorable rest period for a second or two.

In the next year's fifth grade several of the girls were among the most physically fearless children in the entire class. But it was true then, much more than now, that on the matter of admitting or showing fear there was a different code for boys than for girls.

This makes me think about written work. Some say that children get security from large amounts of written work. Maybe. But suppose every teacher in the school were told that he had to do ten pages of addition problems, within a given time limit and with no mistakes, or lose his job. Even if the time given was ample for doing all problems carefully with time over for checking, the chances are that no teacher would get a perfect paper. Their anxiety would build up, as it does in me when I play the flute, until it impaired or wholly broke down their coordination and confidence. Have you ever found yourself, while doing a simple arithmetic problem, checking the answer over and over, as if you could not believe that you had done it right? I have. If we were under the gun as much as the kids in our classes are, we would do this more often.

Perhaps children need a lot of written work, particularly in math; but they should not get too much of it at one time. Ask children to spend a whole period on one paper, and anxiety or boredom is sure to drive them into foolish errors. It used to puzzle me that the students who made the most mistakes and got the worst marks were so often the first ones to hand in their papers. I used to say, "If you finish early, take time to check your work, do some problems again." Typical teacher's advice; I might as well have told them to flap their arms and fly. When the paper was in, the tension was ended. Their fate was in the lap of the gods. They might still worry about flunking the paper, but it was a fatalistic kind of worry, it didn't contain the agonizing element of choice, there was nothing more they could do about it. Worrying about whether you did the right thing, while painful enough, is less painful than worrying about the right thing to do.

Children may get some security from doing a lot of written work, *if,* and only if, they can decide themselves when and how much of this they want to do. When we give children long lists of arithmetic problems to do in school, hoping to create confidence, security, certainty, we usually do quite the opposite, create boredom, anxiety, less and less sharpness of attention, and so, more and more mistakes, and so in turn, more and more fear of making mistakes.

Lore Rasmussen, who became a good friend of Bill's and mine after this book first came out, worked out in her math classes a way in which children could and did get security from written work. She invented many varied and ingenious worksheets (many now commercially available), each one dealing with a particular aspect of math or arithmetic. She had many copies of these in a file drawer, and one copy of each in a master catalog on her desk. Children could look through the catalog, find which worksheet they wanted to work on, get one out of the file, and do it.

Lore soon found that children would very

often do a particular worksheet, *correctly*, half a dozen or more times before deciding that they had done it enough. Children do not drink from dry wells, and these children were not doing these sheets to get good marks or to please Lore—it was their own business. Clearly each time they repeated a worksheet they were learning something new from it, or making more secure what they already knew. When they felt that they really owned that particular bit of knowledge, they stopped and went on to something else.

But most homework, when it is not pure busywork to fill up the children's time, is designed to convince the teacher, not the children, that they know something. And so it rarely does good, and usually does harm.

One way to keep down tension is to be aware of it. I told the math class that to let something go by in class without knowing what it means, and without saying anything, is like leaving something in Howard Johnson's on a long car trip. You are going to have to go back for it eventually, so the sooner the better. This foolish analogy has helped the kids, or so they say. They have learned to recognize, if only a little, the feeling of panicky confusion that slowly gets hold of them. To be able to say, "I'm getting left at Howard Johnson's" helps them to control this feeling, and if it gets too much for them they can always tell me that they have been left behind; then I can do something about picking them up.

We must set a limit to the tension that we put children under. If we don't, they will set their own limits by not paying attention, by fooling around, by saying unnecessarily, "I don't get it." We should let them know in advance that they will not have to be under tension for an entire period, and that, if need be, they have the means to bring it to a stop.

Perhaps this is a reason why people like Gattegno, who go around teaching demonstration math classes, get such spectacular results. The kids know that this is not real school, that this strange man is not their teacher, that if they make mistakes nothing serious will happen, and that, in any case, it will be over soon. Thus freed from worrying, they are ready to use their brains. But how can we run a class from day to day and keep that spirit? Can it be done at all?

☐ **February 5, 1959**

How is it possible for children of only ten to have such strongly developed concepts of themselves, and these unfavorable almost to the point of self-contempt and self-hatred? We expect this of older children; but that it should have gone so far, so soon . . .

Are there any of them who are so busy with the world and with living that they just don't bother to think much about themselves? Perhaps Betty. Perhaps Hal. Not many others.

Perhaps they are thrown too early, and too much, into a crowded society of other children, where they have to think, not about the world, but about their position in it.

I feel this now much more strongly than before.

Is it possible that our modern way of teaching, all
gentleness, persuasiveness, and human contact,
tends to make children get themselves and their
work all mixed up? The first school I went to was
very different from this. Even when I was five, the
teachers there never called me anything but Holt.
Of me, as a person, they seemed to take little notice.
I didn't know whether they liked me or not; it never
occurred to me to wonder. My work was what concerned them. If it was good, it was commended; if
bad, it was criticized. There may be more than we
think in this old-fashioned way of dealing with children. Maybe it was easier for children to grow up in
a world in which, when they impinged on the world
of adults, they were treated firmly, impersonally,
and ceremoniously, but were otherwise left alone.

There was a word on Sam's report card that he
could not understand; he was almost in tears over it.
Why should he have *assumed* that it was bad? Of
course, we adults tend to see all small, specific failures, of our own or of children, as proof of general
failure, incompetence, worthlessness. Is it a cultural
matter? Are there no people in the world for whom
it is not a disgrace to do something badly?

Note the danger of using a child's concept of
himself to get him to do good work. We say "You are
the kind of sensible, smart, good, etc., etc. boy or girl
who can easily do this problem, if you try." But if
the work fails, so does the concept. If he can't do the
problem, no matter how hard he tries, then, clearly,
he is not sensible, smart, or good.

If children worry so much about failure, might it not be because they rate success too high and depend on it too much? May there not be altogether too much praise for good work in the lower grades? If, when Johnny does good work, we make him feel "good," may we not, without intending it, be making him feel "bad" when he does bad work?

Do children really need so much praise? When a child, after a long struggle, finally does the cube puzzle, does he need to be told that he has done well? Doesn't he know, without being told, that he has accomplished something? In fact, when we praise him, are we not perhaps horning in on his accomplishment, stealing a little of his glory, edging our way into the limelight, praising ourselves for having helped to turn out such a smart child? Is not *most* adult praise of children a kind of self-praise? I think of that marvelous composition that Nat wrote about the dining room in his house. I find now, to my horror, that in thinking with satisfaction about that comp, I am really congratulating myself for my part in it. What a clever boy this is! and what a clever man am I for helping to make him so!

☐ **February 11, 1959**

Someone asked the other day, "Why do we go to school?" Pat, with a vigor unusual in her, said "So when we grow up we won't be stupid." These children equate stupidity with ignorance. Is this what they mean when they call themselves stupid? Is this one of the reasons why they are so ashamed of not knowing something? If so, have we, perhaps unknowingly, taught them to feel this way? We should clear up this distinction, show them that it is possible to know very few facts, but make very good use of them. Conversely, one can know many facts and still act stupidly. The learned fool is by no means rare in this country.

Since then I have heard many children, most of them "bright" children in "good" schools, call themselves stupid. By this they mean ignorant—but they also mean unintelligent and beyond that generally worthless, untrustworthy, sure to do the wrong thing. Why did these children believe this of themselves? Because generally adults treated them as if it were so.

At this school children were not allowed to be waiters at lunch tables until fifth grade. The adults who ran the school—many of them psychologists—felt that until children were ten they could not be trusted to carry dishes of food around a room without dropping them, or maybe even throwing them. When children went from one class or building to another, they had to be guided by an adult, in carefully straight lines—one child was always appointed line leader, to help the teacher do this. Without some such system, everyone assumed, the children would never get to where they were going.

As fond of the children as we were, Bill and I shared enough of these prejudices so that when, a few years later, we saw in public schools in Leicestershire, England, six-year-olds carrying dishes of food from kitchen counters to lunch tables, or going from classrooms to assemblies and back again without adult supervision, we were absolutely astonished. When we came home and told people of these marvels, they said, "Well, English kids must be different, you could never get American kids to do that."

It never occurred to any of us that these contemptuous assumptions might be a cause of many of the children's learning problems. To learn much about the world, we must trust it, must believe that it is generally consistent and makes sense. Even more, we must trust ourselves to make sense of it. The world we presented to these children through their schoolwork was a meaningless fragmented world, the parts of it separated from each other, and all of them cut off from any of the children's real experience. And in all the ways in which we dealt with them, we taught them to distrust themselves. Small wonder they used the strategies they did.

As by now many have pointed out, the bad things we assume about other people tend to become true, become "self-fulfilling prophecies."

Many people seem to think that the way to take care of children is to ask in any situation what is the most stupid and dangerous thing the children could possibly do, and then act as if they were sure to do it. One warm April morning I sat playing my cello at the edge of the swan boat pond in the Boston Public Garden. At its edge, the pond is perhaps a foot deep, maybe less. Around it is a broad granite curbing. During the hour and a half I was there, four mothers came by, each with a small child in tow. The youngest of these was about a year and a half old, the oldest close to three. Each of these four children was interested in the water and wanted to go look at it. Each of these four mothers assumed that if the child got anywhere near the water's edge he or she would fall in. They did not shout at their children or threaten them, but each mother rushed about trying to stand between the child and the water, or trying to distract him from the water, or turn him in another direction. Naturally, the more they tried to keep the children away from the water, the more the children struggled to see it, despite the mothers' ever more frantic cries of "No, no, you'll fall in, you'll fall in!"

But all these children were good steady walkers, well past the tottering and falling stage. The odds against their falling into the water, if they had not been harassed and rushed into carelessness and recklessness, would have been, for the youngest child over a hundred to one, and for the older children a million to one.

If these mothers are "careful" this way long enough, they are very likely to get just the behavior they don't want. Little children are indeed very careful at first—watch them on a stair or some steps, deciding whether to step down forwards or crawl down backwards. They are eager to try new things, but at the same time they have a remarkably accurate sense of what they can and cannot do, and as they grow older, their judgment about this improves. But these fussed-over children are almost certain to become either too timid to try anything or too reckless and careless to know what they can try and what they should leave alone.

To prove they are not afraid, they will try to do things that no sensible and careful child would do, and then, having put themselves in danger, they will not be confident and cool enough to get themselves out.

Years ago I visited an adventure playground in Holland Park in London. The playground was full of trees to climb, ropes to swing on, and other "dangerous" stuff. I asked the young people in charge whether many children got hurt there. They said, "No, not since we told the adults that they couldn't come in." When the mothers *could* come in, they were constantly saying "Don't do this, don't do that, it's too dangerous." The children would be so angry and humiliated by this kind of talk that in a spirit of "I'll show you" they would rush to climb a too tall tree or use a too difficult piece of apparatus. Once in danger, with their mothers' "You'll fall, you'll fall" in their ears, they would soon get rattled, and down they would come with a crash. So the people in charge of the playground built a little waiting area where mothers could sit and talk *but could not see their children* while the children used the playground. Since then, they told me, their most serious injury had been one mildly sprained ankle. Left alone, children made very prudent choices about what kind of risks they would run—for being adventurous, of course they wanted to run *some* risks. At the same time, they learned how to be cool and collected in risky situations.

Some people are very unwilling to believe this. The other day, at a meeting about home schooling, I met one such person, an official in some kind of "service" agency, a professional defender of children and provider of compulsory help. She was very angry at all my talk of giving children responsibilities and rights, letting them do serious work—above all, letting them stay home unattended. She insisted they didn't have the judgment to do such things. To prove it she told me a story about her twelve-year-old daughter. She told it in a very strange and contradictory tone of voice. On the one hand, she seemed to be speaking more in sorrow than in anger—"I wish I didn't have to say this, but I have to say it." On the other hand, her voice was full of relish and triumph—"See, this *proves* that children can't be trusted, but must always have people like me (for most people aren't qualified) to look out for them."

The story was that one evening she had dinner cooking on and in the stove. Suddenly she had to go out for a while, and told her daughter to watch the dinner. Details here were vague; it wasn't clear whether she told her daughter to turn off the stove at a certain time, or said that she would be home in time to turn it off, or what. Anyway, when she returned home ten minutes later (so she said), the dinner was burned, the whole house was full of smoke, and heaven knows what other disasters had happened. The story as told is a little hard to believe; if you overcook a dinner for ten minutes you don't usually get a house full of smoke. "See," this woman kept saying in her sorrowful but triumphant voice, "the poor girl did her best, but she's just a *child*, she doesn't have the judgment." Having finally learned when argument is useful and when it is not, I did not ask how much judgment it takes to turn off a stove. Nor did I say, as I would have liked to, "Madam, I don't know what kind of games you and your daughter are playing with each other, or for what reasons, but I know of quite a few children half your daughter's age who can and frequently do plan a meal, buy all the food, and cook it."

This deep lack of trust in children, this feeling that at any second they may do something terribly stupid or destructive, has to some extent poisoned the air of almost every kindergarten, nursery school, or day care center I have seen—and the people who have shown me these places have always thought they were showing me the best. The people in charge, usually very pleasant, kindly, and intelligent young women, are full of this kind of anxiety. However much they might like to, they can never settle down to a relaxed, calm, quiet conversation or game or project with one or two children, but must always be darting nervous glances around the room to be sure that everyone is doing something and that no one is doing something bad. The result is that a child rarely ever gains the full attention of the adults; they are always looking out of the corner of their eye at someone else. Their unease tends to make all the children uneasy, even when they are on the whole doing things they enjoy.

I have seen a great many of these groups of young children in the Public Garden, nursery schools or day care centers out for a picnic or a ride on the swan boats or just a frolic in the air and space and green grass. I almost always take a few minutes to watch the children play. As I do I also look at the adults in charge of these groups. Hardly any of them ever seem to be getting any pleasure from being with the children. Most of them, in fact, look angry, and are constantly saying to the children in sharp and disagreeable voices, "Stand still, be quiet, don't run, stop that, stay close to me." But even the few adults who don't look mean and angry, seldom look happy. They almost never give me the kind of sharing, conspiratorial look that I often get from loving mothers who see me admiring and enjoying the sight of their little children. The women in charge of these groups of children are too worried about all the bad things that might happen to be able to get any pleasure from their small companions. And yet, what could go wrong? The street is far away, with a fence in between, and even if a child made a dash for the street, which I have never seen one do, it wouldn't take an adult more than a few steps to catch up.

It is not the ratio of children to adults in the

group, but the total number of children that seems to determine how anxious are the adults. In this respect a group of thirty children attended by five adults is not at all like a group of six children attended by one adult, for this reason, that in the large group every one of the five adults worries about *all thirty* of the children. The bigger the group, the more the worry, no matter how many adults there may be.

If we could revive our one room schools, with all ages mixed together, competent teachers would not find it hard to manage schools of thirty students. The younger children would learn from those a little older, and the oldest of all, who would look like grownups to the little ones, could help take care of them. But in our giant schools of a thousand or more students, classes of thirty are indeed too big for all but a few teachers to work with. It is schools rather than classes that we need to make smaller.

☐ **April 24, 1959**

Strategy is an outgrowth of character. Children use the strategies they do because of the way they feel, the expectations they have of the universe, the way they evaluate themselves, the classroom, and the demands made on them. Rachel sees the class as a place where she is told to do certain things, praised if she does them right, disapproved of if she does not. She is not likely to use good strategy no matter how much we press it on her. Even if I give her problems which she must think about to solve, and even if she thinks about them and solves them, which hardly ever happens, she will make of this a kind of production strategy. She will say, as I think she does say, that this is a crazy class and that this screwball is always giving her funny kinds of problems to puzzle over; but she will not carry this way of working on problems over into other work, or into the main part of her life. Her first concern will still be self-defense.

One thing we see in our intelligent children is that they are intensely involved with life. Rachel, Pat, Elaine, Garry, all are daydreamers. But Barbara, Betty, Maria, Ralph, and Hal don't withdraw from life; they embrace it. We spoke once of a love affair with learning. These children seem to have a love affair with life. Think of the gusto with which Betty, or Barbara, or Sam tell even the simplest story about themselves.

Intelligent children act as if they thought the universe made some sense. They check their answers and their thoughts against common sense, while other children, not expecting answers to make sense, not knowing what is sense, see no point in checking, no way of checking. Yet the difference may go deeper than this. It seems as if what we call intelligent children feel that the universe can be trusted even when it does not seem to make any sense, that even when you don't understand it you can be fairly sure that it is not going to play dirty tricks on you. How close this is in spirit to the remark of Einstein's, "I cannot believe that God plays dice with the universe."

On page 54 in the July 1958 *Scientific American,* in the article "Profile of Creativity," there is the following apt comparison:

> The creative scientist analyzes a problem slowly and carefully, then proceeds rapidly with a solution. The less creative man is apt to flounder in disorganized attempts to get a quick answer.

Indeed he is! How often have we seen our answer grabbers get into trouble. The fact is that problems and answers are simply different ways of looking at a relationship, a structure, an order. A problem is a picture with a piece missing; the answer is the missing piece. The children who take time to see, and feel, and grip the problem, soon find that the answer is there. The ones who get in trouble are the ones who see a problem as an order to start running at top speed from a given starting point, in an unknown direction, to an unknown destination. They dash after the answer before they have considered the problem. What's their big hurry?

Here are Elaine, the answer grabber, and Barbara, the thinker, at work on the problem $\frac{3}{4} + \frac{2}{5} = ?$

Elaine (adding tops and bottoms, as is her usual custom): Why not $\frac{5}{9}$?

Barbara: $\frac{5}{9}$ is less than $\frac{3}{4}$. She saw that since $\frac{2}{5}$ was added to $\frac{3}{4}$, the answer would have to be bigger than $\frac{3}{4}$; so $\frac{5}{9}$ could not be it. But this went right over Elaine's head.

Elaine: Where's the $\frac{3}{4}$?

Barbara: In the problem!

Yet I doubt that any amount of explaining could

have made Elaine understand what Barbara was saying, far less enable her to do the same kind of thinking for herself.

The poor thinker dashes madly after an answer; the good thinker takes his time and looks at the problem. Is the difference merely a matter of a skill in thought, a technique which, with ingenuity and luck, we might teach and train into children? I'm afraid not. The good thinker can take his time because he can tolerate uncertainty, he can stand not knowing. The poor thinker can't stand not knowing; it drives him crazy.

This cannot be completely explained by the fear of being wrong. No doubt this fear puts, say, Monica under heavy pressure; but Hal is under the same pressure, and maybe I am as well. Monica is not alone in wanting to be right and fearing to be wrong. What is involved here is another insecurity, the insecurity of not having *any* answer to a problem. Monica wants the right answer, yes; but what she wants, first of all, is an answer, any old answer, and she will do almost anything to get some kind of answer. Once she gets it, a large part of the pressure is off. Rachel was like this; so was Gerald, and many others. They can't stand a problem without a solution, even if they know that their solution will probably be wrong. This panicky search for certainty, this inability to tolerate unanswered questions and unsolved problems seems to lie at the heart of many problems of intelligence. But what causes it?

Some might say here that this is all a matter for the psychiatrists. I am not so sure. A person might well be distrustful in personal relationships and still have a kind of intellectual confidence in the universe. Or is this possible? And if so, can it be taught in school?

☐ June 16, 1959

A year ago I was wondering how a child's fears might influence his strategies. This year's work has told me. The strategies of most of these kids have been consistently self-centered, self-protective, aimed above all else at avoiding trouble, embarrassment, punishment, disapproval, or loss of status. This is particularly true of the ones who have had a tough time in school. When they get a problem, I can read their thoughts on their faces, I can almost hear them, "Am I going to get this right? Probably not; what'll happen to me when I get it wrong? Will the teacher get mad? Will the other kids laugh at me? Will my mother and father hear about it? Will they keep me back this year? Why am I so dumb?" And so on.

Even in the room periods, where I did all I could to make the work nonthreatening, I was continually amazed and appalled to see the children hedging their bets, covering their losses in advance, trying to fix things so that whatever happened they could feel they had been right, or if wrong, no more wrong than anyone else. "I think it will sort of balance." They are fence straddlers, afraid ever to commit themselves—and at the age of ten. Playing games like Twenty Questions, which one might have expected them to play for fun, many of them were concerned only to put up a good front, to look as if they knew what they were doing, whether they did or not.

These self-limiting and self-defeating strategies are dictated, above all else, by fear. For many years I have been asking myself why intelligent children act unintelligently at school. The simple answer is, "Because they're scared." I used to suspect that children's defeatism had something to do with their bad work in school, but I thought I could clear it away with hearty cries of "Onward! You can do it!" What I now see for the first time is the mechanism by which fear destroys intelligence, the way it affects a child's whole way of looking at, thinking about, and dealing with life. So we have two problems, not one: to stop children from being afraid, and then to break them of the bad thinking habits into which their fears have driven them.

What is most surprising of all is how much fear there is in school. Why is so little said about it? Perhaps most people do not recognize fear in children when they see it. They can read the grossest signs of fear; they know what the trouble is when a child clings howling to his mother; but the subtler signs of fear escape them. It is these signs, in children's faces, voices, and gestures, in their movements and ways of working, that tell me plainly that most children in school are scared most of the time, many of them very scared. Like good soldiers, they control their fears, live with them, and adjust themselves to them. But the trouble is, and here is a vital difference between school and war, that the adjustments children make to their fears are almost wholly bad, destructive of their intelligence and capacity. The scared fighter may be the best fighter, but the scared learner is always a poor learner.

Early in our work together Bill Hull once said to me, "We've got to be interchangeable before this class." In other words, we mustn't appear to them as the Bill Hull or John Holt we are, but only as whatever kind of teacher we decide, in our private talks, we will be. We soon learned that this could not be done. We were very different people—in some ways, more different than even we knew at the time—and we could not pretend to be the same unless we pretended to be nobody.

But a human being pretending to be nobody is a very frightening thing, above all to the children. I think of a lovely story that a friend of mine told me about her then four-year-old daughter. The house rule on weekends was that when the children woke they could get up, but had to be quiet until Mom woke up. One Sunday the mother was very tired and slept later than usual. For a while the little girl was very good about being quiet. But as time passed, and Mom's ordinary waking up time went by, she began to feel more and more the need for her mother's company. She began to make little "accidental" noises, a toy dropped here, a drawer shut a little too loudly there. In time, these noises woke the mother up. But she thought to herself defiantly that if she just stayed in bed long enough, maybe in time the child would give up and leave her alone. So she lay there pretending to sleep.

Finally the child could stand it no longer. She came to her mother's bedside, and with a delicate thumb and forefinger very gently opened her mother's nearest eye, looked into it, and said softly, "Are you in there?"

Children looking into our eyes do indeed want to know whether we are in there. If we will not let them look in, or if looking in they see nobody there, they are puzzled and frightened. With such adults around, children cannot learn much about the world; they must spend most of their time and energy thinking about the adults and wondering what they will do next.

There is a paradox here. Many of the adults who hide themselves from children, pretending to be some idealized notion of "Teacher," might well say they do this in order to make themselves consistent and predictable to the children. The real me, they might say, is capricious, moody, up one day and down the next. It's too hard for the children to have to deal with that changeable, unpredictable real person. So instead, I will give them an invented, rule-following, and therefore wholly predictable person. And it works exactly backwards. Children, unless they are very unlucky, and live at home with adults pretending to be model parents (which may be a growing trend), are used to living with real, capricious, up-one-day-and-down-the-next adults—and with their sharpness of observation and keenness of mind, they *learn how to predict these strange huge creatures,* and to read all their confusing signs.

They know the complicated emotional terrain of the adults they live with as well as they know their room, their home, their backyard or street. But trying to deal with adults who have tried to turn themselves into some kind of machine is like trying to find your way in a dense fog, or like being blind. The terrain is there, but you can't see it.

Later in the year, when the children and I had become very good friends, one of them told me that she could always tell when I was starting to "get mad." I asked how she knew. "Well," she said, wrinkling up her face as she thought about it, "Your forehead gets kind of orange." Orange, I thought to myself. Then I remembered that when my sister and I were about that age, we could tell when our mother (who usually wore dark glasses) was angry by looking at the skin on *her* forehead; it didn't change color, but it had a kind of stretched, tight look about it that told us to watch out. By the time I taught those fifth-graders I was bald, and my skin was very light and sunburned very easily, so the children, with their sharp eyes, could see even that very faint change of color that told them I was beginning to feel annoyed.

Children can detect and understand these subtle human signs and signals much better than they can figure out our rules—which half the time we don't stick to anyway. When the children in a later fifth-grade class began to be so noisy that it started to trouble me, one of them would very often say in warning, "Look out, he's getting ready to put the Q up!"—the Q being my signal for silence [see pp. 62–67]. They were hardly ever wrong. When they said that, I could never keep from laughing. The sharp little rascals! But by the same token they could usually tell, without my having to say anything, when I was tired, or worried, or somehow out of sorts, and out of consideration more than fear, they would make an effort to be quieter and less demanding than usual.

☐ **August 12, 1959**

This morning, near the end of the children's concert on the Esplanade, I saw, sitting on my right about forty feet away, what looked like a retarded child. Beside her sat her very attractive, suburban-looking mother, and another woman. The child looked about thirteen, though it was hard to tell. She was eating a sandwich, and drinking milk through a straw out of a half-pint carton. Every so often she slowly, deliberately brought the sandwich up to her mouth, took a bite, and chewed it as she lowered the sandwich to her lap. Then she carefully raised the carton, centered the straw exactly, and took a careful sip. One might have thought the carton contained nitroglycerine from her way of handling it. Frequently, she looked briefly and silently at her mother, who was conversing with the other woman and seemed to be paying no attention to her. I realized later that she was looking to see whether what she was doing was all right.

What first struck me about this child, as so often is the case with seriously retarded children, was the extraordinary ugliness of her face. Yet there was nothing especially wrong with her features, except a kind of sick down-turning of the mouth. She could never have been called pretty, but her features were normal and regular, and her coloring normal, though a bit pale and unhealthy looking.

My shock, horror, and pity for her and her mother were so strong as to block any thinking. I concentrated on watching without seeming to watch. She was so intent on her milk and sandwich that she did not notice me. And as I watched an interesting thing happened. The orchestra, which was playing a piece that almost surely she did not know, reached the closing bars, and as it did the girl put down her food, looked toward the orchestra, and raised her hands as if ready to clap. A moment later the piece ended, and hearing others clap, she began to clap.

The concert over, the conductor began to say the usual words, "We're glad you've come. Come again next year, etc." and the girl, without changing the ghastly expression on her face, raised her arm stiffly in what I realized after a while was a gesture of good-bye. She seemed to be going through a ritual. When people are leaving, you wave good-bye. This orchestra was leaving, so she waved good-bye; but not because she was communicating something to the orchestra, only because it was something that she had been trained to do.

As the mother and friend continued to eat and chat, I moved to the shade of a tree, where I could watch unobtrusively. Into my mind there came a conversation I had recently had with a close friend, about the rightness or wrongness of killing deformed children in infancy. He had said that he had always thought he might leave a deformed baby with its face in a pillow, so that its death might look like an accident. I asked whether he thought a wife would ever agree to this, and we agreed that it is something a mother would probably never do.

> Alas for innocence and ignorance. We now know that thousands, tens of thousands of mothers, out of their own frustration and misery, have done and keep on doing far worse things than this to children who are not deformed at all.

At the same time, he felt that to keep such children alive was so terrible for both mother and child that it would be better for the child to be dead.

This conversation, boiling up in my mind, crowded out any thinking about the retarded girl; but after a while I began to think about her again. Why was she so terrible to look at? What is so horrifying about mentally defective children in general? Is it the contrast between what we think of as human qualities and the lack of these qualities in someone of human shape? My mind made a sentence, as if talking to someone: "We have to see someone who is less than human to appreciate what it means to be human."

But then, I thought, there is nothing horrifying about the less than human, about animals, for instance. I suddenly realized that what made this child horrifying to see would have been equally horrifying in an animal. Have you ever seen a dog perpetually scared out of his wits, tail curled between his legs, always looking over his shoulder,

slinking around, shying and leaping at every noise?
That, too, is horrifying. What made this child terrible to see was not that she was less than fully human,
but that she was less than fully animal.

> I have by now seen many more "retarded"
> children, and adults, and they all had this same
> dreadful expression of shame, anxiety, and fear.

When we say a child is retarded, what do we
mean? Why, that she is mentally and emotionally
like much younger children. Yet only a look at the
younger children on the grass, listening, fooling
around, dreaming, playing, teasing, was enough to
show that this poor child, though perhaps mentally
six or seven years old, was like no six-year-old, or
three-year-old, who ever lived.

About this time mother and friend got up, folded
their blanket, and started to walk across the grass in
the opposite direction. As they passed the now empty bandshell, the girl again raised her arm in another stiff wave—and then her mother gently
reached up and drew her hand down again, and, lest
the child think this a rebuke, held her hand as they
walked the rest of the way across the grass. It
seemed to me that she brought the girl's hand down
because to wave at an empty bandshell was inappropriate, the kind of thing a much younger child
might do, might even be petted and admired for.

Let us say that retarded children are children
who, for one reason or another, are slower to learn
the ropes, to pick up what their elders think is
appropriate behavior for their age. What must their
home life be like? I have a mental picture of the life

of this child; I see her, hundreds and thousands of times, doing something which is not bad, not wrong, but just inappropriate for her age, and being told, gently or sorrowfully, not to do it. What a confusion in her mind! It is hard enough for children to learn to do and not to do the things that are really necessary—don't touch, don't run into the street, don't go in the medicine cabinet, etc. If we add to this already long list all the things that a retarded child would be told not to do "because you're too old for that," it is easy to see how such a child's reasoning power and faith in the world could break down altogether.

My point is that retarded children are made, not born. No; I daresay this child really was retarded.

I now suspect that many "retarded" children are indeed made rather than born. The process works like this: First, a child who is not following usual paths or timetables of development is "diagnosed," which is to say labeled, as being defective; secondly, the child is treated as if he or she were defective—all in the name of care, treatment, therapy; thirdly, the child learns to think of himself as defective; and finally, he more and more becomes what the experts said he was.

Years ago I met a wonderful public elementary school teacher in western New York State. Because there was no place else to put him, a boy who had been labeled retarded had been put in one of her classes. The boy was terribly neglected, underfed, filthy dirty, in raggedy clothes, full of fear and shame. This teacher found ways to take care of these physical needs. Then she began to give the boy what he needed even more—courteous attention, physical contact, moral support. Under this kindly treatment, *as so often happens*, the child, who had had virtually no school skills at all, did five or so years worth of schoolwork in one year and caught up with the class.

At this point the teacher went to whoever was in charge of the boy's school records, to get the "retarded" label taken off him. She showed them the evidence that the child had done five or more years of schoolwork in one year, and still other evidence of his intelligence and ability. She took it for granted that the experts would join her in saying "Good! This child isn't retarded, but very able; we're delighted to hear it; what wonderful news! We'll change those records right away." Far from it. Their response was not to defend and help the child it was their job to help, but to defend those other experts whose judgment seemed to be challenged. They refused to take the retarded label off the child. Over and over they said—this teacher spent more than a year trying to remove that label—that she must have made some mistake, that whoever put the label on must have known what they were doing.

The last thing this teacher told me was that the child's family was moving to another city and school district, and that she had written and would keep writing to the school authorities in that district, telling of the fine work the child had done, so that they would not dump him back in retarded classes. How it all came out, I don't know.

What puzzles me is, if IQ measures even roughly the rate at which we learn, why a child with an IQ of 50 should not *in time* get to be a reasonably normal and competent person. It is said that, in terms of what he knows and can figure out, the average adult is not much beyond the level of the average twelve-year-old. For all my skepticism about the measurement and testing of intelligence, I think this reflects some kind of truth. Then why should not the child with the IQ of 50 catch up with the crowd, more or less, by the time he is twenty-five? What happens to him along the way to ensure that he will never catch up?

I don't believe any longer that IQ "measures even roughly the rate at which we learn." What it does is measure, roughly, the rate at which we learn *certain things*—on the whole, things that upper-middle-class children tend to learn and do. Beyond that, IQ tests measure our ability to solve certain kinds of puzzles, usually symbolic and very limited in extent, in a short amount of time. It does not test and never could test what Whitehead said was the most important aspect of intelligence, the ability to ask good questions and to know what questions were worth asking. Nor does it—nor could it—test the ability to work at and eventually solve large and difficult problems over long periods of time. Even when we set aside the heavy culture bias built into the tests, they measure at best only a very narrow and trivial part of the wide range of human intellectual abilities.

So when people tell me that a child is "retarded," I always ask, "How do you know? What is the evidence?" I know one child who did not start talking or walking until after he was three, and whose speech, until after he was five, could hardly be understood except by his own family. Within a very short time and without any special treatment he became a fluent and skillful talker, and one of the most brilliant natural athletes I have ever known.

Our mistake is at bottom a mistake of language. We take the word "normal," meaning *usual,* what happens most of the time, and turn it into *proper, correct, desirable,* what ought to happen all of the time.

What turned this particular child from a girl whose body was too big for her behavior into a kind of monster of fear and tension that would make you sick at heart to watch?

I thought that had she been acting like a normal, healthy child of half her age, she would have been less distressing to watch. Then my mind's eye conjured up a picture of her, romping around at the concert like a six-year-old, and I sensed very vividly the horror that this inappropriate behavior would arouse in all who saw it. So it may well be that the tension we see in retarded children is caused, not so much by their being prevented from doing things that to them seem perfectly natural, as by the horror and revulsion that their inappropriate behavior arouses in all who see it, including, and perhaps above all, their own parents. For we may be sure that, retarded or not, they sense and understand these feelings, which are vastly more effective and terrible than any punishment.

A great deal of the training of retarded children must be aimed at concealing their condition, at making them look as if they were brighter than they are. The child who is mentally six is obliged to play the role of a child of twelve. Like the child this morning, whose entire attention was concentrated on *not spilling* (who would care if a six-year-old spilled something?), they have to think self-consciously about every single thing they do. They must lead lives something like the heroes of stories of impersonation, who, pretending to be someone else, must continually remember to walk, talk, whistle, sing, scratch, move a certain way, *always*, with detection, capture, and death the penalty for forgetting. The task must be enough to break the spirit of all but the most practiced, disciplined, and self-confident adult. Small wonder that it should be far too much for a child who is untrained, fearful, and all too aware of the low opinion most people have of him. Even the impersonator, the spy, gets a rest now and then; the mentally six-year-old trying to act twelve hardly ever does. The picture is almost too nightmarish to think about. Perhaps I exaggerate; but then, remembering the fact of this child, I think not. It would take a living nightmare to make that kind of haunted face.

If adult intolerance of behavior that to these kids

seems natural makes terrified monsters out of what began as merely slow children, what are we to do? We have to draw some line between behavior approved and disapproved, or how is the child to learn? But the great difference between the normal child and the retarded child is that the former is punished for his "bad" behavior; the latter may not be punished, but he is abhorred, which is far worse.

Is it possible that such exaggerated adult reactions to children's misbehavior may tend to make juvenile delinquents? The other day I was walking across Boston Common when I saw two boys having a spitting contest. This in itself would fall far outside the bounds of what most adults would consider tolerable. Why are we so sensitive to spitting? It didn't bother me that much, so I walked closer to see who was winning and to get the reactions of other passers-by. Then the smaller boy began to do something that overshot my bounds of the tolerable. He began to spit at the other boy. He wasn't a very good shot, and didn't hit him; but it upset me. I was further upset by his voice, which was loud, harsh, hoarse, gravelly, with the hysterical overtones of someone always on the edge of a fight. Then they noticed me watching, and with one voice started saying, "Hey, mister, gimme a nickel to ride home, etc." I wanted no more to do with them, and walked away. I regret the reaction, but in the same case I would probably react that way again.

There must be children, and this small boy might well be one of them, who, being of stronger character than our poor retarded girl, react differently to the shock and horror which their behavior rouses in adults. Far from making themselves sick with anxiety trying to avoid rousing this horror in adults, these kids look for ways to rouse it. They recognize that their ability to shock and horrify is a kind of power over other people.

If strong disapproval of children's behavior makes neurotics at one end and terrorists at the other, what should we do? Perhaps the answer is to give both kinds of children things to use their human powers on that will be more interesting than either their fears or the possibility of arousing fear in others. Not that this will be easy to do; but it is where we should aim.

□ **October 3, 1959**

Yesterday, three young boys were riding the subway to Park Street. They were exceedingly noisy, excited, and rude. They may not have been "delinquents," but they looked as if they could have been, and certainly as if they wanted the rest of us to think they were. The sudden contact with them was shocking. They seemed so far from what we are used to in people, so close to wild animals—but that is a libel on animals. It was hard not to feel that there was no open door through which they could be reached. About them in the car was an aura of stiff and anxious resentment, which they seemed to recognize and enjoy. People were mentally drawing their skirts and coattails aside.

As I watched these boys, I began to see them as they were. Each time one of them said or did something to shock the people in the car, he looked quickly and anxiously at the faces of his companions, to see whether he had won their approval. Then it would be the turn of another to try to outdo him in noisiness and rowdiness, and to look for his approval in turn. It was suddenly clear that these boys were alone, anxious, frightened, and ready to do anything, anything at all, that would, if only for a moment, gain them the approval of their fellows. For their security they had nothing but each other, and they were so anxious that they had almost no security to give. Every time one of them laughed at another's joke, his laughter was almost instantly cut short by the need to do something that would make the other laugh at him. Their approval of each other almost instantly soured into jealousy.

What did these boys have to nourish their self-respect and self-esteem besides the short-lived and uneasy approval they gave each other? Only the palpable disapproval of everyone else around them, a disapproval close to fear. If you can't make people like you, it is something to be able to make them afraid of you.

Harrison Salisbury, in *The Shook-Up Generation,* and Warren Miller, in *The Cool World,* describe, the former as reporter, the latter as novelist, the world of the delinquent. It appears from what they say that even in the most tightly knit street gangs there is little of what we could call friendship. Gang members are no more than uneasy allies, welded together partly by fear of the world outside and partly by the certain knowledge that nobody else in the world gives a damn about them.

□ **December 14, 1959**

It often seemed last year as if Garry was deliberately turning back from the world of success, which was strange to him, and which, though it offered new and sweet rewards, might also contain hidden dangers, in favor of the world of failure in which, even if he was not very happy, he was at least at home. Today I saw, more clearly than ever before, why failure, unrelieved and total, may seem to some students to be a promising strategy for school and even for life.

Trudy is bright, has a keen sense of the ridiculous, and is more or less the class screwball. Her schoolwork is very poor, by any standards, her spelling perhaps worst of all. On her papers she spells worse than an average third-grader. During the first part of the fall her spelling did not improve at all. Finally, after many struggles and failures—everything I learn about teaching I learn from the bad students— I have come up with some ideas that seem to help, even with the poor spellers.

When a child misspells a word on a paper, I print the word correctly with Magic Marker on a 3×5 card. The children use these like a tachistoscope. By moving a blank card quickly over the printed card, I give them a split second look at the word, then ask them to spell it. They can have as many looks as they want; but each one is very short. This prevents them from spelling the word aloud in their heads, and then trying to remember what they "said." I want them to use their eyes to see what a word looks like, and their mind's eye to remember what it looks like.

The bad spellers, of course, accumulate quite a

stack of cards. I tell them that if they spell one of these words correctly on a surprise test, I will remove it from their cards. They all enjoy reducing their piles of spelling cards, which seem to hang over their heads a little. Today I gave Trudy a surprise test. It was a surprise for me; she got about twenty words right out of twenty-five. What surprised me most of all, when she had finished this good performance, was to see her looking, not pleased or satisfied, but anxious. I thought, "Becoming a better speller presents risks to this child. What on earth can they be?" And then I saw why for some children the strategy of weakness, of incompetence, of impotence, may be a good one. For, after all, if *they* (meaning we) know that you can't do anything, *they* won't expect you to do anything, and *they* won't blame you or punish you for not being able to do what you have been told to do. I could almost hear the girl saying plaintively to herself, "I suppose he's going to expect me to spell right all the time now, and he'll probably give me heck when I don't."

Children who depend heavily on adult approval may decide that, if they can't have total success, their next-best bet is to have total failure. Perhaps, in using the giving or withholding of approval as a way of making children do what we want, we are helping to make these deliberate failers. I think of a sixteen-year-old boy I once knew who, unable to fulfill all his father's very high expectations for him, decided to fulfill none of them. The father was a pillar of the community, good at everything he did; the boy became a playboy and a drunk. One night, at a party, the father was watching his son doing a very drunken and quite funny tango alone in the middle of the dance floor, before a laughing and admiring crowd. The thought flashed through my mind, "Well, that's one thing he can do better than you can."

It is often said that alcoholics may be very able people who feel they cannot meet the high standards they have set for themselves, and hence don't try. Perhaps children find, or try to find, in hopeless incompetence the kind of refuge that an alcoholic finds in liquor. But how do we get children to kick the failure habit? Do we organize a society of Failers Anonymous?

Incompetence has one other advantage. Not only does it reduce what others expect and demand of you, it reduces what you expect or even hope for yourself. When you set out to fail, one thing is certain—you can't be disappointed. As the old saying goes, you can't fall out of bed when you sleep on the floor.

□ **January 3, 1960**

Some people say that it is bad to read old-fashioned fairy tales to little children, because they make them afraid. But even without fairy tales, the lives of little children are full of fears. Like very primitive people, they live in a world that they cannot begin to understand. Fairy tales could do for small children, and indeed did for many years, what myth, ritual, and religion did for primitive peoples—give their fears a name and an identity, a handle to take hold of and perhaps to cast them out by. A child who can channel his fear of the unknown into a fear of ghosts, witches, ogres, giants, wicked fairies, and the like, may be able to rid himself of much of that fear when he finds that such things do not exist. Even if not, he will have had practice in dealing with fear, in facing and thinking about what he is afraid of.

A small boy I knew, when he was about four, used to tell to any sympathetic listener endless stories about his particular monster, which he called a Mountain-Lion-Eater. I suppose he had begun with stories about a mountain lion, that being the fiercest thing he could think of, and had later learned enough about real mountain lions to feel that they were not large or terrible enough to contain all the fear and terror that he wanted to put into them. But something that ate mountain lions!—that might just fill the bill. And this was no ordinary monster. He ate up not only mountain lions but houses, neighborhoods, cities, even the whole world when he was in the mood. In some stories, the little boy overcame the monster; in others, the monster ate him up. It all depended on how he felt at the moment. In either case, his private mythology did him a great service by enabling him in part to see from outside and acknowledge his courage or his fear.

□ **July 20, 1960**

My seventeen-month-old niece caught sight of my ball-point pen the other day, and reached out for it. It has a plastic cap that fits over the point. She took hold of it, and after some pushing and pulling, got the cap off. After looking it over, she put it back on. Then off again; then on again. A good game! Now, if

I want to be able to use my pen, I have to keep it out of sight, for when she sees it, she wants to play with it. She is so deft in putting it back on that it makes me wonder about all I've read about the lack of coordination in infants and the imprecision of their movements. Under the right circumstances—when they are interested—they may be much more skillful than we think.

These quiet summer days I spend many hours watching this baby. What comes across most vividly is that she is a kind of scientist. She is always observing and experimenting. She is hardly ever idle. Most of her waking time she is intensely and purposefully active, soaking up experience and trying to make sense out of it, trying to find how things around her behave, and trying to make them behave as she wants them to.

In the face of what looks like unbroken failure, she is so persistent. Most of her experiments, her efforts to predict and control her environment, don't work. But she goes right on, not the least daunted. Perhaps this is because there are no penalties attached to failure, except nature's—usually, if you try to step on a ball, you fall down. A baby does not react to failure as an adult does, or even a five-year-old, because she has not yet been made to feel that failure is shame, disgrace, a crime. Unlike her elders, she is not concerned with protecting herself against everything that is not easy and familiar; she reaches out to experience, she embraces life.

Watching this baby, it is hard to credit the popular notion that without outside rewards and penalties children will not learn. There are some rewards and penalties in her life; the adults approve of some things she does, and disapprove of others. But most of the time she lives beyond praise or blame, if only because most of her learning experiments are unobserved. After all, who thinks about the meaning of what a baby is doing, so long as she is quiet and contented? But watch a while and think about it, and you see that she has a strong desire to make sense of the world around her. Her learning gives her great satisfaction, whether anyone else notices it or not.

This idea that children won't learn without outside rewards and penalties, or in the debased jargon of the behaviorists, "positive and negative reinforcements," usually becomes a self-fulfilling prophecy. If we treat children long enough *as if* that were true, they will come to believe it is true. So many people have said to me, "If we didn't make children do things, they wouldn't do anything." Even worse, they say, "If *I* weren't made to do things, *I* wouldn't do anything."

It is the creed of a slave.

When people say that terrible thing about themselves, I say, "You may believe that, but I don't believe it. You didn't feel that way about yourself when you were little. Who taught you to feel that way?" To a large degree, it was school. Do the schools teach this message by accident, or on purpose? I don't know, and I don't think they know. They teach it because, believing it, they can't help acting as if it were true.

☐ **February 26, 1961**

The unbelievable incompetence of some of the kids sometimes drives me wild. They can't find anything. They have no paper or pencil when it's time for work. Their desks are a mess. They lose library books. If they do homework at home, they leave it there; if they take home material to do homework, they leave the assignment at school. They can't keep their papers in a notebook. Yet they are not stupid or incapable children; they do many things well.

Ted is an intelligent, alert, curious, humorous, and attractive boy, with a record of unbroken failure and frustration in school. He is an excellent athlete, strong, quick, and well coordinated. But his school papers are as torn, smudged, rumpled, and illegible as any I have ever seen. The other day the class was cleaning out desks, and I was "helping" him. We got about a ream of loose papers out of the desk, and I asked him to put them in the notebook. As always, when he is under tension, his face began to get red. He squirmed and fidgeted, and began to mutter. "They won't fit, the notebook's the wrong size"— which wasn't true. Finally he assembled a thick stack of papers and began to try to jam them onto one of the rings in his notebook, not noticing that the holes in the papers were at least a half-inch from the ring. As he pushed and fumbled and muttered, I felt my blood pressure rising until, exasperated almost to rage, I said loudly, "For heaven's sake, leave it alone, do it later, I can't stand to watch any more of it!"

Thinking over this scene, and many others like it, I was suddenly reminded of a movie, *A Walk in the*

Sun, based on the novel by Harry Brown. It showed the adventures of a leaderless platoon of infantrymen during the first days of the invasion of Italy. At one point, while the platoon is moving through some woods, they are surprised by an enemy light tank, which, amid a good deal of confusion, they manage to ambush. When this action is over the soldiers find that their sergeant, who has been growing rapidly more anxious, and is clearly the victim of battle fatigue, has given way completely. They find him hugging the ground, shaking all over, babbling incoherently. They leave him behind as they move inland toward their vaguely conceived objective. One of the soldiers remarks as they go that the sergeant has finally dug himself a foxhole that they can't get him out of.

It seems to me that children dig themselves similar foxholes in school, that their fumbling incompetence is in many ways comparable to the psychoneurotic reactions of men who have been under too great a stress for too long. Many will reject this comparison as being wildly exaggerated and inappropriate. They are mistaken. There are very few children who do not feel, during most of the time they are in school, an amount of fear, anxiety, and tension that most adults would find intolerable. It is no coincidence at all that in many of their worst nightmares adults find themselves back in school. I was a successful student, yet now and then I have such nightmares myself. In mine I am always going to a class from which, without the slightest excuse, I have been absent for months. I know that I am hopelessly behind in the work, and that my long absence is going to get me in serious trouble, of what sort I am not sure. Yet I feel I cannot stay away any longer, I have to go.

It is bad enough to be a teacher and feel that the children in your charge are using the conscious and controlled parts of their minds in ways which, in the long run and even in the short, are unprofitable, limiting, and self-defeating; to see them dutifully doing the assigned work and to be sure that they are not getting a scrap of intellectual nourishment out of it; to know that what they seem to have learned today they will have forgotten by next month, or next week, or even tomorrow.

But it is a good deal worse to feel that many children are reacting to school in ways that are not under their control at all. To feel that you are helping make children less intelligent is bad enough, without having to wonder whether you may be helping to make them neurotic as well.

☐ **March 2, 1961**

A woman who has spent many years working with children with severe learning blocks, children whom conventional schools, even in slow sections, could not deal with at all, told a class of teachers the other day that early investigators of children who could not read coined the term "word blindness" to describe what they saw. There has been much talk about word blindness since. The experts of the moment seem to believe that the cause is neurological, that there is in a certain percentage of children something in the organization and structure of the brain which makes word recognition difficult or impossible.

Perhaps this is the cause of some reading problems, but that it is the only or the most frequent cause is open to grave doubt. My own belief is that blindness to patterns or symbols, such as words, is in most instances emotional and psychological rather than neurological. It is a neurotic reaction to too great stress. I have often experienced it myself.

The most severe case came during a flute lesson. I describe it in some detail because the kind of tensions that are needed to bring about this loss of the ability to see meaningfully are such that, except in time of war or extreme danger, most adults are not likely to experience them.

The lesson was in the late afternoon. I had had a difficult and discouraging day in class, followed by a tense and unpleasant committee meeting. I was late in leaving, was delayed by heavy traffic, and arrived late for my lesson, with no chance to warm up. My teacher had also had a trying day, and was not his usual patient self. He was exasperated that I had made so little progress since the previous lesson, and began, as exasperated teachers do, to try by brute will power to force me to play the assigned passage as fast as he thought I should be able to play it.

The pace was much too fast; I began to make mistakes; I wanted to stop, but cowed by his determination, hesitated to make the suggestion. A feeling of physical pressure built up in my head. It felt as if something inside were trying to burst it open, but also as if something outside were pressing it in. Some kind of noise, other than my miserable playing, was in my ears. Suddenly I became totally note-blind. The written music before me lost all meaning. *All* meaning. It is hard to describe what I felt. It lasted no more than a second or two, only as long as it took me to stop playing and look away from the music. I could see the notes, but it was as if I could not see them. It is said of such moments that everything becomes a blur. This may have been true; when to go on seeing clearly becomes unbearably painful, the eyes may well refuse to focus. There was also an impression that the notes were moving and shifting on the page. But above all else was the impression that, whatever I was seeing, it was as if I had never seen such things before, never heard of them, never imagined them. Any and all associations they might have had for me were, for that instant, destroyed. They were completely disconnected from all my previous experience.

These sensations were indescribably frightening and unpleasant. After a second or two, I put down my flute and turned away from the music. My teacher sensed that I had been driven over the edge of something, and after a short rest, we went on at a more relaxed pace. But suppose I had been a child? Suppose I had not been free, or felt free, to turn away? Suppose my teacher had felt that it would be good for my character to force the pace harder than ever?

Since the book first came out, a number of people, some of them professional musicians, have told me they have had the same experience.

And as I described in the early part of *Never*

Too Late, I have often had it myself, usually when trying to play my part in an orchestra going too fast for me. In some way the mind is unable to see the notes in a way that can get meaning from them. But also, to some extent the mind may be *refusing* to see them.

During the seven and a half years in which I have been playing the cello, I have been for the most part a very poor sight reader. When I look at a new piece of music, even a piece which I will soon be able to play, I can't just play it the first time I look at it, not at any proper tempo. I have to figure out what the notes are telling me to do with my hands.

I read music the way bad readers, or beginning readers, read print. This is a strange and interesting experience for me, because I learned to read print when very young, and could soon read fluently, almost without thinking about it. Only in music do I know what it *feels* like to be a bad reader.

Musicians have said to me, as I say to readers of print, that the best way to become a better reader is not to worry and to read more. It works. I am still not a good sight reader, but I am getting better.

Musicians also tell me not to read one note at a time, but to read groups of notes, whole measures, phrases—the "words" of music. For a long time I have tried to do this, but it has been very hard for me. I *try* to read groups of notes, but I can't, I can only *see* one note at a time.

The other day I was reading through a string

quartet I am working on, when I noticed, to my great surprise and pleasure, that every so often I could see several notes at once, sometimes even, if the notes were not too thick, a whole measure. It was not a matter of *trying* to see them. I just saw them. They were there. I couldn't see them before, now I can. What has happened?

What I suspect has happened is that as my anxiety has gone down my peripheral vision has gone up—I can see more things at once. Anxiety, fear, tension seem to narrow the range of things I can see or attend to. I don't know where this narrowing takes place, in the eye itself, at the retina, whether it has something to do with the amount and complexity of information that can be passed from the optic nerve to the brain, or whether it has to do with how much of that information the brain can turn into perception. But there seems to be good evidence that increasing anxiety narrows that range.

George Leonard, writing about sports, made a nice distinction between what he called "hard" and "soft" vision. We use hard vision when we look at something through a microscope, or telescope, or at a ball we are trying to hit. We use soft vision to see what is going on over a large part of our field of vision, like a basketball player (Leonard's example) who can see everything happening on the court at once, or a quarterback who can see all his receivers, instead of having to look first for one, then another, or a broken field runner who can see everyone downfield who is coming at him, and how fast they are coming, and from what angle. When people asked O. J. Simpson how he "knew" how to make his brilliant open field runs, he used to say, like all great running backs who are asked that question, that he didn't know, he just saw everything and it was as if the path were laid out for him.

This ability to take in and make use of a lot of information at once seems to me a very high indicator of intelligence in the broadest sense. It led me to say once, at a conference at which someone had made some sneering remark about basketball players, that it probably took more real intelligence to play good basketball than to write the average Ph.D. thesis. This produced a very mixed reaction.

If we could find a way to raise and lower anxiety at will, and measure it instantaneously, we could probably design experiments that would show that the range of our attention narrows dramatically as we become more anxious. In any event, I know that as I grow less anxious about reading music, my range of attention is increasing.

The other thing my musical friends used to tell me to do was read ahead, keep my eyes a little bit ahead of the notes that my hands are playing. When reading print aloud I can easily do this; my eyes are always a little ahead of my voice. But I haven't been able to do in music what I can easily do in print.

There were two reasons for this, one obvious, the other less so. The obvious reason was that every time I played a note the teacher or the mistake corrector in my head would say "Are you sure that was the right note?" In other words, I was always thinking about the note I had just played, instead of the note I was about to play. Correcting that habit was mostly a matter of being aware when I was doing it, and in learning ways (which I won't go into here) to stop doing it.

But even when I was not, so to speak, looking behind the music, behind the notes my hands were doing, I found it very hard to look ahead. Some of this was anxiety, which made it impossible to have two thoughts in my head at once. But there was something else, that I only discovered a few weeks ago. Reading a new piece of music, a hard piece for me, I became aware that my eyes were glued to the note I was playing. I made a conscious effort to look a little bit ahead, but found it very difficult; it roused a lot of anxiety. I examined my own thoughts and feelings about this. I found two things. First, I was afraid that if I looked away from the note I was playing I would not be able to find it again, would be "lost," would have to send my eyes all over the music on a frantic search for my place.

This feeling, that if I took my eyes off the note I could not find it again, led to an even stranger and more irrational feeling, that the note was actually *trying to get out from under my eye*, that if I did not, so to speak, *pin* the note to the paper with my eye, it would get away. I was so astonished to discover this feeling that I laughed out loud. Ridiculous to think such a thing! But I could tell that I really had thought it from the great relief, pleasure, and excitement that I felt when I discovered it.

Now, knowing this, if I catch myself trying to pin notes to the paper with my eye, I say to myself, "Come on, that's just ink on the page, it isn't going to move." To the extent that I can really convince myself that I can take my eyes off the note and then go back and find it right where I left it, I can make my vision a lot softer. Now and then I can do something, did it last night while working on the Dvorak "American," as a matter of fact, that I would not have dared try to do or been able to do only a little while ago. Seeing a number of measures ahead that were obviously all alike, I looked to the end of them to see what came next. I felt as I did it that I was taking a small risk. But it worked; at the slow tempo at which I was playing, I could actually play one thing and look ahead to another.

I mention all this only to make the point that bad readers of print almost certainly have a similar feeling, that if they take their eye off the word, even the very letter that they are looking at, it will jump out from under their eye, somehow escape from the page, and they will never be able to find it again. These feelings must be all the more severe in children who are made to read aloud in front of others, and who are scolded or made terrible fun of by the other children and the teacher if they lose their place.

It is good practice for me to read my cello part while listening to a recording of the same music. I can practice looking away from the note being played and then looking back to it. In the same way, it might be very helpful to many children if they could, as (thanks to cassettes) many of them do, hear a book being read aloud while they look at the same book themselves.

This is of course one of the things that happens when parents read aloud to little children, holding them on their laps or close beside them. Some of the time, children no doubt follow word by word the words they are hearing. But at other times their eyes wander, they look ahead, look even to the end of the page to see how far away it is, and then look and find the "right" place again. And so, without knowing that they are doing it, they learn an important skill of reading, and one which could not be learned in any situation where much anxiety was present.

☐ **March 5, 1961**

Some people say of nonreaders, "These children can't or don't read because of the way they use their minds." Others retort, "No; they don't read because of the kind of minds they have." The argument seems to me unreal as well as useless. The distinction between what our minds are and how we use them is one that exists only for purposes of talk; it does not exist at the level of reality. The mind is not a kind of thinking machine that someone or something inside of us uses, well or badly. It *is;* and it works, perhaps well, perhaps badly; and the way it works one time has much to do with the way it will work another time.

Religious mystics in India, so we are told, stand for many years with an arm raised, or a limb distorted or immobilized in some fashion. After a while the limb becomes unusable. What sense does it make to argue whether the cause of this is physical, or lies in the way the limb was used? It was the way it was used that made it the kind of limb it was, a limb that could not be used any other way. It is probably true of the mind as well, that the way we use it determines how we can use it. If we use it badly long enough, it will become less and less possible to use it well. If we use it well, the possibility grows that we may use it even better. We must be wary, then, of assuming that because some learning difficulties seem to be caused by brain dysfunction they are therefore incurable. The brain, as an organ, may have far more flexibility and recuperative powers than we realize. What it cannot accomplish one way it may be able to do another. Conversely, we must be aware of the extent to which, in causing children to make poor use of their minds, we may be making their minds less and less useful to them.

□ **March 21, 1961**

Today Andy had a long, tough session with me. He finally solved the problem I had given him. But I can't help wondering what he learned. Not much; he certainly didn't gain any insight into the property of multiplication in which I was interested. All that he had to show for his time was the memory of a long and painful experience, full of failure, frustration, anxiety, and tension. He did not even feel satisfaction when he had done the problem correctly, only relief at not having to think about it anymore.

He is not stupid. In spite of his nervousness and anxiety, he is curious about some things, bright, enthusiastic, perceptive, and in his writing highly imaginative. But he is, literally, scared out of his wits. He cannot learn math because his mind moves so slowly from one thought to another that the connections between them are lost. His memory does not hold what he learns, above all else because he won't trust it. Every day he must figure out, all over again, that $9 + 7 = 16$, because how can he be sure that it has not changed, or that he has not made another in an endless series of mistakes? How can you trust any of your own thoughts when so many of them have proved to be wrong?

I can see no kind of life for him unless he can break out of the circle of failure, discouragement, and fear in which he is trapped. But I can't see how he is going to break out. Worst of all, I'm not sure that we, his elders, really want him to break out. It is no accident that this boy is afraid. We have made him afraid, consciously, deliberately, so that we might more easily control his behavior and get him to do whatever we wanted him to do.

I am horrified to realize how much I myself use fear and anxiety as instruments of control. I think, or at least hope, that the kids in my class are somewhat more free of fear than they have been in previous classes, or than most children are in most classes. I try to use a minimum of controls and pressures. Still, the work must be done—mustn't it?—and there must be some limits to what they can be allowed to do in class, and the methods I use for getting the work done and controlling the behavior rest ultimately on fear, fear of getting in wrong with me, or the school, or their parents.

Here is Andy, whose fears make him almost incapable of most kinds of constructive thinking and working. On the one hand, I try to dissipate those fears. But on the other, I have to do something to get him to do the work he so hates doing. What I do boils down to a series of penalties, which are effective in exactly the proportion that they rouse the kind of fears that I have been trying to dispel. Also, when children feel a little relieved of the yoke of anxiety that they are so used to bearing, they behave just like other people freed from yokes, like prisoners released, like victors in a revolution, like small-town businessmen on American Legion conventions. They cut up; they get bold and sassy; they may for a while try to give a hard time to those adults who for so long have been giving them a hard time. So, to keep him in his place, to please the school and his parents, I have to make him fearful again. The freedom from fear that I try to give with one hand I almost instantly take away with the other.

What sense does this make?

□REAL LEARNING

Memo to the Math Committee: _____
We tell children here to think about the meaning of
what they are doing. We say this is the sure way to
the right answer. But it may lead instead into one of
the paradoxes and contradictions of which elementary math is full. In such cases the student who
thinks, as I used to, "Oh, well, I'll just do what they
tell me, and not worry about it," can often move on
without difficulty, while the one who thinks hard
about what he is doing can get into a tangle from
which neither he nor his teachers may be able to
free him.

One of the fifth-grade groups was trying to discover how to divide by fractions. They had been given,
to figure out for themselves if they could, "Divide 6
by ½." The children know the official school definition of division, that "8 divided by 4" means either
"How many 4's are contained in 8?" or "If you
separate 8 into 4 equal parts, how many will be in
each part?" Most of the group applied the first
meaning of division to the problem, taking it to
mean, "How many ½'s are contained in 6?" They

saw that the answer was 12. But two girls, who had done excellent thinking about multiplying fractions only a few days before, tried to apply the other meaning of division, and asked themselves: "If you divide 6 into halves, how big will each half be?" Quite reasonably, they got the answer 3.

It was their good thinking, and my bad, that got them into difficulty. I had not told them that the second of the two meanings of division did not apply, and was in fact without meaning in the case of division by a fraction. The reason I had not told them is that I had not realized it myself. Since I had given them the rule, they felt that it must make sense, and in fact twisted it to make sense in the only way it could be made to make sense. Six divided into half a part could only mean six divided into halves.

My misuse of language reinforced their misunderstanding. Like most people, I frequently use the word "divide" in a way that contradicts its mathematical meaning. We say: "Divide a pie into four parts" when all we are really doing is making two perpendicular cuts through the center of the pie; we say, "Divide a line into two parts," when what we mean is to find the midpoint of the line; we talk about dividing something in half when it would be more consistent to talk about dividing it in two. For all these reasons it was natural for these girls to suppose that dividing 6 by ½ meant dividing it into halves, or two parts.

One able boy unwittingly increased their confusion. Early in the period he explained at the blackboard that the problem was asking how many ½'s were contained in 6, and showed with a good diagram that the answer was 12. Then he made a mistake that many adults might easily have made. He said, "Twelve what?" Then, after a second's thought, he answered, "Twelve halves," and wrote $12/2$ on the board. He soon saw his mistake, and corrected it; but too late to save the girls. They had seen a leading member of the opposition go to the board, and using the other meaning of division, prove that 6 divided by $1/2$ is $12/2$, or 6. Since this was nonsense, they were all the more convinced that their own answer was right.

Other children began to try to show the girls where they had gone wrong, but without success. To rescue a man lost in the woods, you must get to where he is. The other children could not get to where these girls were, could not see how they had arrived at their answer, and hence could not help them. All they could do, like most teachers, was repeat over and over again how they got their own answer—which was no help at all. One boy asked one of the girls to work out $6 \times 1/2$ on the board. She wrote, "$6 \times 1/2 = 3$." He then pointed out that they had just said that 6 *divided* by $1/2$ equaled 3. The girl looked at her partner and said, "We've been tricked!" I wonder how often we, their teachers, make them feel this way.

Here one girl began to feel that the answer 3 was somehow wrong, and whispered to her partner, "We goofed." Later she said, "one half of 6 is the same as multiplication." She still could not see clearly that what she was doing was multiplying, not dividing. Finally, after much further argument, she said to her partner, "We may as well give in. Half of 6 is 12. I don't get it, but it is."

These words threw a sharp light on the world of school as seen through the eyes of children. How much of my teaching has been accepted by the children in just this spirit? What I tell a child may seem to contradict his common sense, the common usage of English, and even other things I have told him; but he must bow to superior force and accept it whether it makes sense or not.

I was finally able to get the girls out of their jam, and admitted my own responsibility for getting them into it. But I had been thinking and talking for some weeks about possible contradictions in my own teaching, and so was particularly sensitive to it. This incident shows that we teachers must begin to try to look at our ideas and our teaching through the eyes of someone who knows nothing, can accept nothing unproven, and cannot tolerate inconsistency and paradox. We must try to free our teaching from ambiguity, confusion, and self-contradiction. Since to bring clarity and consistency to "elementary" mathematics is one of the central mathematical problems of our time, this task will not be easy.

☐ **July 28, 1958**

One day, some years ago, some friends said, "Ever seen any silicone putty?" I said I had never even heard of it. They gave me a lump. I kneaded it, flattened it, stretched it into a long thin piece, tore it into smaller pieces. Then they said, "Roll it into a ball, and throw it on the floor." I did so. My eye, and my brain, and my very bones knew what would happen—the putty would splat on the floor and stick. I threw it, and while my eye, so to speak, stayed stuck to the floor the putty bounced up as high as my head. For an awful split second, the universe rocked around me. I was on the brink of terror. Then, in this same instant, something wrenched in my mind, something said, "Okay, so it bounces, very funny, what'll they think of next?" and I was back in the world of order and reason.

This makes me think of the little girl—first-grader? second-grader?—who burst into tears the other day when her teacher told the class how to spell "once." The teacher probably assumed that the child cried because the word was so hard. The chances are that she cried because the word was so crazy, because it smashed into pieces the understanding that she had been carefully building up in her mind about the way words are spelled. Even then, she could probably have lived with this crazy word if only the teacher had troubled to point out that it was crazy. What really makes school hard for *thinkers* is not just that teachers say so much that doesn't make sense, but that they say it in exactly the way they say things that are sensible, so that the child comes to feel—as he is intended to—that when he doesn't understand it is his fault.

What seems simple, natural, and self-evident to us may not seem so to a child. Take, for example, the numeral 10. We are so used to it that we cannot imagine what it might be like, knowing what 1 and 0 stand for, to be told that when you put them together it stands for something much bigger than either of them. We should acknowledge the obvious *nuttiness* of this when we first present this numeral to children, so that they will not feel on the outside of a baffling mystery. Otherwise this first encounter with 10 may give children a shock from which they never fully recover, and which freezes up their minds every time they think about it.

> But children who are teaching themselves how to read, as many do, do not burst into tears when they see the word "once," or any one of hundreds of other words that don't sound the way they look. Children who are learning on their own, learning what interests them, *don't* get all upset everytime they meet something unusual or strange. To young children, everything is strange. They may think and fantasize a great deal about what they do not understand, but they worry about it very little. It is only when other people, adults, start trying to control their learning and force their understanding that they begin to worry about not understanding, because they know that if they don't understand, sooner or later they are going to be in some kind of trouble with those adults.
>
> In the same way, children will not be shocked and frightened by the nuttiness, the paradox of the numeral 10, if they are free to get to know that numeral 10 as they might get to know another child—seeing as much of 10 as they want, thinking about it only when they want. One day they will know 10, it will suddenly stop seeming strange, and they may wonder why they ever thought it was strange.

Nobody "explained" 10, or the function of base and place in our numeral systems, when I was little. I went to a very old-fashioned school where they just showed you how to do problems without ever trying to explain why they did them that way, or to convince you that this made any sense. This was probably hard on the children who weren't very good at parroting. But I was great at parroting, and the advantage for me of this system was that I was left alone to make sense of 10, and a lot of other things, in my own time and my own way.

Bad explanations are a great deal worse than no explanations at all.

☐ **November 13, 1958**

Kids have trouble with arithmetic, not only because they have to memorize a host of facts that seem to have no pattern, meaning, or interest, but also because they are given a host of rules for manipulating these facts, which they have to take on faith. I don't continually have to check my arithmetic operations against the world of numbers, because I have proved to my satisfaction that the rules for manipulating numerals have their roots in the world of real quantities and really work there. I know I can safely use the conventional method to multiply 24×36 because I know that this means the same thing as $(20 \times 30) + (4 \times 30) + (20 \times 6) + (4 \times 6)$. But if I didn't know that this was true, what sense would the conventional system of multiplication make? How could I feel that this mysterious business of "bringing down the zero" and "moving the next line over" would give me the right answer? How could I ever check it against reality and common sense?

The beauty of the Cuisenaire rods[1] is not only that they enable the child to discover, by himself, how to carry out certain operations, but also that they enable him to satisfy himself that these operations really work, really describe what happens.

> "The beauty of the rods . . ." I am very skeptical of this now. Bill and I were excited about the rods because we could *see* strong connections between the world of rods and the world of numbers. We therefore assumed that children, looking at the rods and doing things with them,

[1]Since I will be describing the work of children with the Cuisenaire rods, a word about them is in order. Named after their inventor, a Belgian schoolteacher, they are a set of wooden rods, or sticks, one centimeter (cm) wide and one cm high, about the thickness of one's little finger; they vary in length from 1 cm to 10 cm (1 cm = about ⅜"). Each length of rod is painted its own color: 1 cm—white; 2 cm—red; 3 cm—light green; 4 cm—crimson (often called "pink" by the children); 5 cm—yellow; 6 cm—dark green; 7 cm—black; 8 cm—brown; 9 cm—blue; 10 cm—orange.

In writing about the use of the rods, I will often call them by their colors; but I will put their length in centimeters as a reminder, thus: yellow (5).

Anyone particularly interested in children's work with arithmetic would probably do well to get a set of the rods, so that they may use them to see for themselves what some of the children I describe were actually doing. For information about the rods, write to Cuisenaire Co. of America, Inc., 12 Church St., New Rochelle, New York 10805, or Caleb Gattegno, Educational Solutions, 80 Fifth Ave., New York, New York 10011.

Though the rods were invented and first used by Cuisenaire, their use has been greatly expanded and refined by Dr. Caleb Gattegno, a British professor of mathematics and psychology, who introduced them into many other countries, including the United States, where they are used (and misused) in a rapidly increasing number of schools.

could see how the world of numbers and numerical operations worked. The trouble with this theory was that Bill and I *already* knew how the world of numbers worked. We could say, "Oh, the rods behave just the way numbers do." But if we *hadn't* known how numbers behaved, would looking at the rods have enabled us to find out? Maybe so, maybe not. Clearly they helped some children, in our classes and elsewhere. Clearly they did not help many others. Just as clearly, many or most of the teachers who at one time or another tried to use the rods did not understand them or use them well. The rods had not made the world of numbers and operations with numbers clear to them; naturally they could not use the rods to make these things clear to their students.

☐ **November 26, 1958**

Do the Cuisenaire rods give us as much control over bad strategy as we like to think? Is there not a chance that some of the strategists may not still be slipping something over on us? I imagine a student, like our old friend Emily. I say, "What is the 3 of the 4?" *"Three fourths."* "What is the four of the three?" *"Four thirds."* "What is the 4 of the 5?" *"Four fifths."* "What is the 5 of the 4?" *"Five fourths."* Sure, I ask children to look at the rods as they do this. But do the rods themselves determine the answer? Might not the students be playing a word-shoving game with us? Suppose I said to Emily,

"What is the blip of the blop?" Might she not answer, *"Blip blopths"?* "What is the blop of the blip?" *"Blop blipths."* Isn't this a perfectly good strategy? It gives right answers. I suspect that Caroline and Monica are doing just this, and I heard Gil say the other day something about "You take the one that comes first . . ." Merely telling them to hold on to the rods and look at them will not frustrate this strategy.

One way of dealing with these strategists is to vary the form of our questions. We might hold up a yellow (5) rod and say, "If this is 1, show me ⅗"; or "If this is 2, show me 4." Such questions might test more fully whether they were really seeing the rods and their relationships.

Isn't there something to be said for asking, whenever possible, questions that can be answered without words? Questions that can be answered by doing something, showing us something?

"Questions that can be answered . . ." This was not a bad idea as far as it went, but it did not go far enough. Asking children questions that required them to do something, rather than merely say something, was still no improvement if, having tried to do what we asked, they still had to depend on us to tell them whether they had done it right. What we needed were tasks with an evident goal, like puzzles—unlock the rings, make the ball go in the hole, etc. No one ever asks "Have I done this jigsaw puzzle right?"

I'll say more about this later when I talk about the Math Laboratory.

☐ **December 6, 1958**

Observing in Bill Hull's Class: _____
The other day you were doing that business with the
kids in which you hold up two rods and ask what one
is of the other. I noticed after a while that you
always asked, first, what the small one was of the
large. The children answered with a fraction in
which the smaller number was the numerator. I
noticed then that if you paused, or looked doubtful,
or repeated the question, some of them quickly
reversed their answer. If they had said five sevenths,
they then said seven fifths. Three people did this:
Rachel, one of the boys, and Barbara.

It was Barbara who really made the dent on me,
because she is usually such a thoughtful and capable
student. You held up the black (7) and the blue (9)
and, reversing your previous procedure, said, "What
is the blue of the black?" She said, "Seven ninths."
You hesitated. Her face got red, she stared at you,
not at the rods, for a second and then said, "Nine
sevenths." Nothing in her face, voice, or manner
gave me the feeling that she had the slightest idea
why the first answer was wrong and the second
right, or even that she was sure that the second was
right. If *she* is not sure, I don't like to think about
the others.

We want the rods to turn the mumbo-jumbo of
arithmetic into sense. The danger is that the mumbo-jumbo may engulf the rods instead. It doesn't do
any good to tell Monica to look at the rods if she
doesn't believe that when she looks she will find the
answer there. She will only have two mysteries to
contend with instead of one.

☐ **December 7, 1958**

One day in math class I was trying to make the point that division is not just a trick that we carry out with numerals, but an operation that could be done even by someone who didn't know any numerals. I asked the children to suppose that they had a large bag of marbles, which they wanted to divide as evenly as possible among four people, and furthermore that they had no way of counting them. Most of the children realized that by giving out a marble at a time to each person in turn until all the marbles were gone they could do the job. But Pat and one other kid had a different idea. Here is Pat's paper.

> You could measure the bag with a ruler, and say it measures to be 8 so then you would measure 2 inches of the bag for each one because there are four people and 2 × 4 is 8 so you measure four 2 inch marks and then you could cut on each 2 inch line like this [small picture here of a bag of marbles with four lines going down it, evenly spaced] and give each person as much as from one 2 inch line to another.

The other one said the same thing in different words. One at a time, I spoke to them. To each I said, "Imagine that I have a big bag of marbles in my hand" (business of showing, by gestures, what a large, heavy bag of marbles would look and feel like). Then I said, "Now in this other hand I have some scissors" (imitation of scissors). "Now I hold the bag in this hand, and I bring the scissors over, and I start cutting this bag in half (gesturing of cutting); what is going to happen?" At this point Pat said "Oh!"; the other child laughed. Then they both said that the marbles would go all over the floor. Only then did they realize that their answer to the problem of dividing up the marbles didn't make any sense.

But of course if those children had had *in real life* the problem of dividing up a bag of marbles among four people, they never would have been so stupid as to try to cut the bag in four parts. Only in school did they think like that.

This brings to mind something that happened when I was in prep school. A friend was studying for a chemistry test. He was trying to memorize which of a list of salts were soluble in water. Going through the list, he said that calcium carbonate was soluble. I asked him to name some common materials made of calcium carbonate. He named limestone, granite, and marble. I asked, "Do you often see these things dissolving in the rain?" He had never thought of that. Between what he was studying for chemistry and the real world, the world of his senses and common sense, there was no connection.

☐ **February 6, 1959**

I have a hunch. Suppose we ask the children to draw two lines, one of them five sevenths of the other. They will probably draw a 5-inch and a 7-inch line.

But then suppose we ask them to draw two more lines, one of them five seventeenths of the other. I wonder how many of them will come up after a while and say it can't be done, because they can't get a 17-inch line on their paper.[1]

Perhaps we can say of understanding that the better we understand something, the more places we can use it. If so, then one way to get children to understand fractions may be to think of as many ways as possible to have them use fractions.

I feel myself beginning to understand the difference between fractions as quantities and fractions as operators. The expression ½ + ⅓ = ⅚ can mean that ½ of 1, plus ⅓ of 1, equals ⅚ of 1. Or it may mean that ½ of something, plus ⅓ of that same thing, equals ⅚ of that same thing, whatever the thing is.

But wait a minute. Are not all numbers operators? When we say 2 + 3 = 5, do we not mean that 2 somethings plus 3 somethings equal 5 of those things? In short, when we teach arithmetic, are we not always teaching algebra whether we know it or not? And may not some of our difficulties and confusions arise from the fact that we don't know it, are not aware of it? When we write 2 + 2 = 4, what we really mean is $2x + 2x = 4x$.

We are used to the idea that we cannot add fractions unless we have common denominators. But this is true of whole numbers as well. Example: 2 horses + 3 horses = 5 horses; but 2 horses + 3 freight trains = what? 5 objects, 5 things, perhaps.

[1] Almost all of them said just this.

But then, we have given horses and freight trains the common denominator, objects.[1]

I have long suspected that there is more to this business of "understanding" arithmetic than meets the eye, and I am just now beginning to get an inkling of how much more. There is nothing particularly simple about "simple" arithmetic. The idea that any nice, sympathetic woman can, without further thought, teach children to "understand" arithmetic is just plain foolish.

> We soon found out that the idea that people with Ph.D.'s in mathematics could teach children to "understand" arithmetic turned out to be just as foolish. Here and there the professor-led revolution in math teaching turned up a few small good ideas. For the most part, though, it did little to improve the teaching of mathematics and in many places may have made it worse.
>
> I doubt very much if it is possible to *teach* anyone to understand *anything*, that is to say, to see how various parts of it relate to all the other parts, to have a model of the structure in one's mind. We can give other people names, and lists, but we cannot give them our mental structures; they must build their own. Many people claim that any field of knowledge or experience can be turned into a series of questions and answers—programmed learning. An

[1]Three years later, and without having given the children any preparation, I wrote on the blackboard of a first-grade class: 2 horses + 3 cows = ? A number of the children gave me the answer "5 animals."

eleventh-grader who had been taught a year or two of programmed math pointed out to me one day, with more insight than he perhaps realized, the flaw in that method: "If people give me the questions I can remember most of the answers, but I can never remember the questions." Exactly.

☐ **March 8, 1959**

The doctrine of this school seems to be that if children make pictures to illustrate their work with fractions, they will understand what they are doing and will not make mistakes. The other day I saw an interesting example of this theory in operation. Pat had the problem $\frac{1}{2} + \frac{1}{3} = ?$ She thought about it for a while, then drew two rectangles, each divided in thirds. She shaded two sections of one rectangle, and wrote, "This is $\frac{1}{2}$." Then she shaded one section of the other, and wrote, "This is $\frac{1}{3}$." She looked at them a bit; then she wrote "$\frac{1}{2} + \frac{1}{3} = 1$ whole." And she sat back with a pleased and satisfied look on her face.

Hester wrote, "$\frac{1}{2} + \frac{1}{3} = \frac{3}{4}$." Barbara, sitting next to her, instantly said, "No! $\frac{1}{3}$ isn't the same as $\frac{1}{4}$." It took me a second or two to see what she meant. Since $\frac{1}{2} + \frac{1}{4} = \frac{3}{4}$, $\frac{1}{2} + \frac{1}{3}$ cannot equal $\frac{3}{4}$. This child looks at everything she does from several different angles to see whether it fits together and makes sense. But how rare, how very rare she is.

I asked Monica the other day how many thirds were in one whole. She said, "It depends on how big the whole is." If we could look into the minds of our students, in how many would we find that thought? They know it is *wrong* and mustn't be said; but how many think it in silence?

Sometimes Pat is in touch with the real world. I asked her, "Would you rather have one third or one fourth of something to eat?" She said in a flash, "Depends what it is."

Right after vacation, I gave everyone in the afternoon section rods and asked them to figure out what ½ + ⅓ would be. I don't remember giving them any hints; I'm almost sure I did not. Most of the class, without hints, shuffled the rods around until they found or made a 6-cm or 12-cm length, found half of it and a third of it, added them, and gave me the answer ⅚. I am almost afraid to try it again. Some of them might be able to do this without the rods; most of them, not.

Betty said, "²⁄₄ + ⅗ is 1 or more. You need two more fifths to make 1, and ²⁄₄ is more than ²⁄₅, so the answer must be bigger than 1." A remarkable kid. And yet, in a conventional school, she might have been considered a "slow" pupil, and might have become one.[1] She *likes* to look at things from several angles, to consider the meaning, or meanings of what she is doing before she does it. But on the whole, this is not the way to get ahead in school.

Later she asked someone, "What's a third of 20— without any halves?"

Still later, they were working on ½ + ¼, and I heard these remarks:

Ralph: It's ¾, and don't ask us how we did it.

[1]Later, some of her math teachers *did* consider her a slow pupil.

Gil: Add 1 and 1 and you get 3?

Betty: I'm not doing it *that* way, I'm doing it *the* way.

Later, working on $\frac{1}{5} + \frac{3}{10}$:

Betty: Answer is $\frac{5}{10}$ or $\frac{1}{2}$.

Gil: But 5 isn't half of 10 and 10 isn't half of 3.

Jane said thoughtfully to herself, "Eight goes into 24 three times. Three goes into 24 how many times?" It took her a long time to figure this out.

Incidentally, in spite of the school crusade against "goes into," all the children say it, without exception.

☐ April 24, 1959

If children come to feel that the universe does not make sense, it may be because the language we use to talk about it does not seem to make sense, or at least because there are contradictions between the universe as we experience it and as we talk about it.

One of the main things we try to do in school is to give children a tool—language—with which to learn, think, and talk about the world they live in. Or rather, we try to help them refine the tool they already have. We act as if we thought this tool of language were perfect, and children had only to learn to use it correctly—i.e., as we do. In fact, it is in many ways a most imperfect tool. If we were more aware of its imperfections, of the many ways in which it does not fit the universe it attempts to describe, of the paradoxes and contradictions built into it, then we could warn the children, help them see where words and experience did not fit together, and perhaps show them ways of using language that would to some extent rise above its limitations.

Look at adjectives—some are, so to speak, absolute: round, blue, green, square. But many others are relative: long, short, thin, thick, heavy, light, high, low, near, far, easy, hard, loud, soft, hot, cold. None of these have any absolute meaning. Long and short only mean longer and shorter than something else. But we use these words as if they were absolutes. In fact, there must be many times when a child hears a particular thing called long one day and short the next, or hot one day and cold the next. We use words as if they were fixed in meaning, but we keep changing the meanings. The soup that has become cold is still too hot for the baby. The short pencil today is the long pencil tomorrow. The big kitty's name is Midnight; but don't be rough with him, he's too little. Horses are big animals; see the little horsie (three times the size of the child). How big you've grown; you can't have that, you're too little. Children adjust to this kind of confusion; but is it an intellectually healthy and useful adjustment, or just a kind of production strategy? Would it be useful to talk to first-graders about why we call a certain mountain small and a certain kitten big? Or is this easy stuff for them?

The conventional teaching of grammar adds to the confusion. We talk about, and use, nouns and adjectives as if they were very different, but in fact they are often very much alike. A green ball, a green top, a green bicycle, and a green stuffed animal are alike in that they are green (adjective) and that they are toys (noun). When we call them green, we mean they are members of a class that have in common the color green. When we call them toys we mean that they are members of a class that have in common the fact that children play with them. Why should a child be expected to feel that there is something very different about these classes? Why is the green-ness of a ball different from the ball-ness of a ball? I don't feel the difference. They are both ways of saying something about the object. We tell children that the distinction between one part of speech and another is a matter of meaning, when it really has to do with the way we fit them into sentences.

☐ **April 30, 1959**

Nat said the other day, when asked how he did a certain problem with fractions, "I find it almost always has some diagonal form." He was looking for a rule to fit all cases with no thought of what fractions actually represent. Elaine, given fractions to add, still adds the tops and the bottoms (+ means add, so when you see a +, you add everything in sight).

I watched Nat working on $\frac{1}{3} + \frac{1}{4} = ?$ He started writing equivalent fractions for $\frac{1}{3}$: $\frac{2}{6}$, $\frac{4}{12}$, $\frac{8}{24}$, etc. Using this doubling process, he wrote a long string of fractions. Then he did the same for $\frac{1}{4}$: $\frac{2}{8}$, $\frac{4}{16}$, $\frac{8}{32}$. But he couldn't figure out why he couldn't get a common denominator for both fractions. Sam had to show him that $\frac{1}{4}$ could be written as $\frac{6}{24}$.

Rule following! Some of these kids are like a man

traveling across open country in a tank. They look out at the world through a tiny peephole, point themselves at a target and start off, but if a bump throws them off course and they lose sight of the target, they're lost. They don't know where they started from, how far they have gone, or where they are.

A first-grader was doing a page of problems in a workbook. The answers were given, but some were right, others not, and the child was supposed to mark them accordingly. He marked the first three or four correct, then put an X by the next one. He did it so quickly that the teacher asked how he knew it was wrong. He said, "Oh, they always put a wrong one about here."

Children's rules. I see nothing wrong any more with these children's attempts to find rules for working with fractions, even if some of those rules seem pretty wild. After all, Kepler, as he tried for about twenty-five years to find the laws governing the motion of the planets round the sun, made some wild guesses of his own. The trouble with the children was that they had no way of finding out whether their rules worked. They could not use either reality or internal logic and consistency as a way of checking them. Instead, they took their work to the teacher and said, "Is this right?"

Furthermore, the rules they invented themselves were so wild, so haphazard, so unconnected with anything, that even when they stumbled on a rule that worked, i.e., got some teacher to say "That's right," they could rarely remember the rule, or what kinds of problems it was supposed to work with.

□ **June 15, 1959**

Kids in school seem to use a fairly consistent strategy. Even the good students use it much of the time, the bad students use it all the time, and everyone uses it when they feel under pressure. One way of describing this strategy is to say that it is answer-centered rather than problem-centered. The difference can best be seen by comparing the way in which the two kinds of people deal with a problem.

The problem-centered person sees a problem as a statement about a situation, from which something has been left out. In other words, there is in this situation a relationship or consequence that has not been stated and that must be found. He attacks the problem by thinking about the situation, by trying to create it whole in his mind. When he sees it whole, he knows which part has been left out, and the answer comes almost by itself. The answer to any problem, school problem, is in the problem, only momentarily hidden from view. Finding it is like finding a missing piece in a jigsaw puzzle. If you look at the empty space in the puzzle, you know the shape of the piece that must fill it.

But most children in school are answer-centered rather than problem-centered. They see a problem as a kind of announcement that, far off in some mysterious Answerland, there is an answer, which they are supposed to go out and find. Some children begin right away to try to pry this answer out of the mind of the teacher. Little children are good at this. They know, especially if they are cute-looking, that if they look baffled or frightened enough, teacher will usually tell them what they need to know. This is called "helping them." Bolder children are ready to sally forth into Answerland in a kind of treasure hunt for the answer. For them, the problem is an answer-getting recipe, a set of hints or clues telling them what to do, like instructions for finding buried pirate treasure—go to the big oak, walk a hundred paces in line with the top of the church steeple, etc. These *producers* think, "Let's see, what did I do last time I had problem like this?" If they remember their recipes, and don't mix them up, they may be good at the answer-hunting game, and the answers they bring home may often be right ones.

Take the problem "Ann is three years older than Mary, and their ages add up to 21. How old is each?" The problem-centered person tries to make these girls real in his mind. Are they grown up? No; their ages will add up to too much. They have to be about 10. All but a few of the possible Anns and Marys disappear, and the correct pair looms up larger and larger, until there they are, aged 9 and 12.

The problem-centered person may use a formula. He might see very quickly that Ann's and Mary's ages added up to twice Mary's age, plus three. He might even write down something like $A + M = 21; M + M + 3 = 21; 2M = 18;$ so $M = 9$ and $A = 12$. But the point is that he would get this formula, this problem-solving process, *out of the problem itself,* not out of his memory.

The answer-centered person, on the other hand,

the skilled one, not the coaxer of teachers or the reader of teachers' minds, thinks, "Now let me see, how are we supposed to do this kind of problem? When did I have one like it? Oh, yes, I remember, you write down something about their ages, let's see, let x equal Mary's age, then we have to let Ann's age be something, I guess $x + 3$, then what do we do, add them together, maybe, yes, that's right, $x + x + 3 = 21$, then we have to transpose the 3, how do we do that, subtract from both sides ..." and so on until he gets an answer which he takes to the teacher and says, "Is this right?" But this answer was *elsewhere,* not in the problem, and the answer-getting process had to be dredged up out of blind memory.

Practically everything we do in school tends to make children answer-centered. In the first place, right answers pay off. Schools are a kind of temple of worship for "right answers," and the way to get ahead is to lay plenty of them on the altar. In the second place, the chances are good that teachers themselves are answer-centered, certainly in mathematics, but by no means only there. What they do, they do because this is what they were or are told to do, or what the book says to do, or what they have always done. In the third place, even those teachers who are not themselves answer-centered will probably not see, as for many years I did not, the distinction between answer-centeredness and problem-centeredness, far less understand its importance. Thus their ways of teaching children, and, above all, the sheer volume of work they give them, will force the children into answer-directed strategies, if only because there isn't time for anything else. I have noticed many times that when the workload of the class is light, kids are willing to do some thinking, to take time to figure things out; when the workload is heavy, the "I-don't-get-it" begins to sound, the thinking stops, they expect us to show them everything. Thus one ironical consequence of the drive for so-called higher standards in schools is that the children are too busy to think.

The other day I was working with a sixteen-year-old boy who was having trouble with first-year physics. I asked him to do one of the problems in his book. Immediately he began to write on his paper

    Given:
    To Find:
    Use:

He began to fill in the spaces with a hash of letters and figures. I said, "Whoa, hold on, you don't even know what the problem is about; at least think about it before you start writing down a mess of stuff." He said, "But our teacher tells us we have to do all our problems this way." So there we are. No doubt this teacher would say that he wants his students to think about problems, and that he prescribed this form so that they would think. But what he has not seen, and probably never will see, is that his means to the end of clearer thinking has become an end in itself, just part of the ritual mumbo-jumbo you have to go through on your answer hunt.

When kids are in a situation where they are not under pressure to come up with a right answer, far less do it quickly, they can do amazing things. Last fall, about November, I gave the afternoon section some problems. I said, "You have never seen problems like these, you don't know how to do them, and I don't care whether you get them right or not. I just want to see how you go about trying to do them." The problems were basically simple algebra problems, like the one about Ann and Mary, or a certain number of nickels and dimes adding up to 85 cents—the kind of problem that many first-year algebra students find so difficult. These fifth-graders tore into them with imagination, resourcefulness, and common sense—in a word, intelligently. They solved them in many ways, including some I hadn't thought of. But it was about that time that the school began to worry about my going too slowly. Soon I was told to speed up the pace, which I am ashamed to say I did, and the children lapsed right back into their old strategies. Probably for keeps.

☐ **October 1, 1959**

Not long ago Dr. Gattegno taught a demonstration class at Lesley-Ellis School. I don't believe I will ever forget it. It was one of the most extraordinary and moving spectacles I have seen in all my life.

The subjects chosen for this particular demonstration were a group of severely retarded children. There were about five or six fourteen- or fifteen-year-olds. Some of them, except for unusually expressionless faces, looked quite normal; the one who caught my eye was a boy at the end of the table. He was tall, pale, with black hair. I have rarely seen on a human face such anxiety and tension as showed on his. He kept darting looks around the room like a bird, as if enemies might come from any quarter left unguarded for more than a second. His tongue worked continuously in his mouth, bulging out first one cheek and then the other. Under the table, he scratched—or rather clawed—at his leg with one hand. He was a terrifying and pitiful sight to see.

With no formalities or preliminaries, no icebreaking or jollying up, Gattegno went to work. It will help you see more vividly what was going on if, providing you have rods at hand, you actually do the operations I will describe. First he took two blue (9) rods,[1] and between them put a dark green (6), so that between the two blue rods and above the dark green there was an empty space 3 cm long. He said to the group, "Make one like this." They did. Then he said, "Now find the rod that will just fill up that space." I don't know how the other children worked on the problem; I was watching the dark-haired boy. His movements were spasmodic, feverish. When he had picked a rod out of the pile in the center of the table, he could hardly stuff it in between his blue rods. After several trials, he and the others found that a light green (3) rod would fill the space.

Then Gattegno, holding his blue rods at the upper end, shook them, so that after a bit the dark green rod fell out. Then he turned the rods over, so that now there was a 6-cm space where the dark green rod had formerly been. He asked the class to do the same. They did. Then he asked them to find the rod that would fill that space. Did they pick out of the

[1]See footnote, p. 138.

pile the dark green rod that had just come out of that space? Not one did. Instead, more trial and error. Eventually, they all found that the dark green rod was needed.

Then Gattegno shook his rods so that the light green fell out, leaving the original empty 3-cm space, and turned them again so that the empty space was uppermost. Again he asked the children to fill the space, and again, by trial and error, they found the needed light green rod. As before, it took the dark-haired boy several trials to find the right rod. These trials seemed to be completely haphazard.

Hard as it may be to believe, Gattegno went through this cycle at least four or five times before anyone was able to pick the needed rod without hesitation and without trial and error. As I watched, I thought, "What must it be like to have so little idea of the way the world works, so little feeling for the regularity, the orderliness, the sensibleness of things?" It takes a great effort of the imagination to push oneself back, back, back to the place where we knew as little as these children. It is not just a matter of not knowing this fact or that fact; it is a matter of living in a universe like the one lived in by very young children, a universe which is utterly whimsical and unpredictable, where nothing has anything to do with anything else—with this difference, that these children had come to feel, as most very young children do not, that this universe is an enemy.

Then, as I watched, the dark-haired boy *saw*! Something went "click" inside his head, and for the first time, his hand visibly shaking with excitement, he reached without trial and error for the right rod.

He could hardly stuff it into the empty space. It worked! The tongue going round in the mouth, and the hand clawing away at the leg under the table doubled their pace. When the time came to turn the rods over and fill the other empty space, he was almost too excited to pick up the rod he wanted; but he got it in. "It fits! It fits!" he said, and held up the rods for all of us to see. Many of us were moved to tears, by his excitement and joy, and by our realization of the great leap of the mind he had just taken.

After a while, Gattegno did the same problem, this time using a crimson (4) and yellow (5) rod between the blue rods. This time the black-haired boy needed only one cycle to convince himself that these were the rods he needed. This time he was calmer, surer; he knew.

Again using the rods, Gattegno showed them what we mean when we say that one thing is half of another. He used the white (1) and red (2), and the red and the crimson (4) to demonstrate the meaning of "half." Then he asked them to find half of some of the other rods, which the dark-haired boy was able to do. Just before the end of the demonstration Gattegno showed them a brown (8) rod and asked them to find half of half of it, and this too the dark-haired boy was able to do.

I could not but feel then, as I do now, that whatever his IQ may be considered to have been, and however he may have reacted to life as he usually experienced it, this boy, during that class, had played the part of a person of high intelligence and had done intellectual work of very high quality. When we think of where he started, and where he finished, of the immense amount of mathematical territory that he covered in forty minutes or less, it is hard not to feel that there is an extraordinary capacity locked up inside that boy.

It is the tragedy of his life that he will probably never again find himself with a man like Gattegno, who knows, as few teachers do, that it is his business to put himself into contact with the intelligence of his students, wherever and whatever that may be, and who has enough intuition and imagination to do it. He has not done much work with retarded children, but he saw in a moment what I might have taken days or weeks to find out, or might never have found out: that to get in touch with the intelligence of these children, to give them solid ground to stand and move on, he had to go way, way back, to the very beginning of learning and understanding. Nor was this all he brought to the session. Equally important was a kind of respect for these children, a conviction that under the right circumstances they could and would do first-class thinking. There was no condescension or pity in his manner, nor even any noticeable sympathy. For the duration of the class he and these children were no less than colleagues, trying to work out a tough problem—and working it out.

The point of this incident may be misunderstood; indeed, *is* being misunderstood. Many people, reading of Gattegno's work with these boys, will think I am saying that if Gattegno could have just spent enough time with them, he could have made them smart. That is not my point at all. What I am saying is that they were *already* smart. What Gattegno did, for an hour or so, was to put within their reach a miniature universe on which they could exercise the intelligence they already had, a universe in which they could do real things and see for themselves whether what they had done worked or not.

Many people, having finally realized that human intelligence in any broad and important sense is not fixed but highly variable, may be and indeed are drawing the wrong conclusion that we can now set out to "teach" intelligence just as we used to try to "teach" math or English or history. But it is just as true of intelligence as it has always been true of school subjects that teaching—"I know something you should know and I'm going to make you learn it"—is above all else what *prevents* learning.

We don't have to *make* human beings smart. They are born smart. All we have to do is *stop* doing the things that made them stupid.

Ingenious teachers, "gifted" teachers, teachers who are good at thinking up new and better ways to teach things, can do just about as much harm to their students as the teachers who are content to plug along with the standard workbooks and teachers' manuals. These gifted teachers *can't stop teaching.* They are like someone who tries to help a friend start a car by giving it a push. He grunts and strains, the car gets rolling, the engine catches and begins to run. The driver says, "It's going now, you can let go." *But the pusher won't let go.* "No, no," he says, "you can't go without me, the car won't go unless I keep pushing." So the car, now ready to run at full speed, is held back—unless

the driver wants to break free and leave the
helper on his face in the road. And most learners, children above all, *can't* break free of their
teachers.

The inventors of clever teaching ideas tend to
think that if one good teaching idea helps to
make some learning happen, a hundred good
ideas will make a hundred times as much learning happen. Not so. A hundred good ideas may
stop the learning altogether.

It took me a long time to learn, as a classroom
teacher, that on the days when I came to class
just bursting with some great teaching idea,
good things rarely happened. The children,
with their great quickness and keenness of perception, would sense that there was something
"funny," wrong, about me. Instead of being a
forty-year-old human being in a room full of
ten-year-old human beings, I was now a "scientist" in a room full of laboratory animals. I was
no longer in the class to talk about things that
interested me, or them, or to enjoy what I and
they were doing, but to try something out on
them. In no time at all they fell back into their
old defensive and evasive strategies, began to
give me sneaky looks, to ask for hints, to say "I
don't get it." I could see them growing stupid in
front of my eyes.

By the time I was teaching my last fifth-grade
class, I usually knew enough, when I saw this
happening, to back off and drop my big project
and go back to our more normal, natural, honest
classroom life. If I had some sort of gadget that I

thought might interest the children, I would leave it in a corner of the room and say nothing about it until someone said "What's that, what's it for, how do you work it?" Or if there was some kind of activity I wanted to "expose" them to, I would do it myself, without saying anything. I assumed that whatever did not interest me would probably not interest them, and was not trying to seduce them into doing things that I myself found boring. But if there were things I liked to do and could do in the classroom, I often did them there.

☐ **February 14, 1960**

I gave Edward a handful of rods and asked, "How many whites would you need to make this many?" He arranged the rods in 10-cm rows, making 15 rows of 10 with a crimson (4) left over. Then he began to count the rows, counting by tens—a sensible procedure—saying, as he touched each row, "10, 20, 30 . . ." and so on up to 100. Then, to my utter astonishment, he said, as he touched the remaining five rows of 10 and the crimson, "200, 300, 400, 500, 600, 604."

I asked him to try again. He assumed that he had made a mistake. This time he counted, as before, up to 100, then, as he touched the remaining rows, said, "101, 102, 103, 104, 105, 109." But he did not look satisfied with this.

The next time Edward began to count the rows of 10, he said, "I'll call each one of these rows 1."

However, when he got to the tenth row of 10, he called it 1000, and called each additional row 100, so that his answer was in the 1500's. After fiddling with this a bit, he went back to his original system, and after getting the answer 604 several times, said with assurance that it was right.

I split the group of rods into two sections, ten rows of 10 in one, five rows of 10, and the crimson, in the other. I asked how much was in each group. After counting, he said there was 100 in the large group, and 54 in the small. I slid the two groups together and asked how many there were in all He went through his usual routine and said again, "604."

What I should have realized at this point is that my *question* was meaningless to him. I thought I was using the rods to test his ideas of number. From his answers I now see that there was little or no connection between the rods and his ideas of number, whatever they were.

I should add that Edward was a very unsuccessful student, way behind grade level in all subjects, above all in arithmetic. If he had been able to do school arithmetic well I wouldn't have meddled with his understanding.

What I might have done, should have done, wish I had done, was give him a huge stack of white rods and ask him to find out how many white rods he would need to make as long a row as he could make with the rods I had on his desk. What I also might have done, and should have done, since I could not get a large quantity of white (1-cm) rods, was to find a meter stick or meter/centimeter measuring tape, which Edward could then have used to check his ideas about the rods. But first it might have been at least helpful and probably necessary—assuming, that is, that this work I was doing with Edward was worth doing at all—to have helped him discover or at least feel sure of the fact that a given quantity of white (1-cm) rods, say six of them, could in fact make a row 6 cm long, or as long as the 6-cm rod. The point of the rods was that they were a concrete way of matching up the idea of number as quantity—six of this, five of that—with the idea of length—6 cm long, 5 cm long. This was obvious to me, but it was probably not obvious to Edward at all.

What he understood my question to mean, what he thought I was asking him to do, I'll never know. He knew I had asked a question that required him to reply with a number. He knew that certain of the rods were associated with numbers. His idea, I guess, was to combine those numbers in different ways to see if he could come up with some number that would satisfy me, be the "right" answer to my meaningless question. There was no way in which he could use the reality he perceived through his senses either to find the right answer or to test the rightness of any answers he gave. It was another year before I was able to think up some problems in which children really could test their thinking against reality. More on this later.

I took away the crimson rod, again split the rods into a group of 100 and a group of 50, and asked how many were in each. Again he told me there were 100 in the large group and 50 in the small. When I slid them together, he told me there were 600.

I then put out 100. "How many are there?" "100." I added a white rod, and asked, "How many now?" "101." I added another white rod and asked, "How many now?" "102." And so up to 109. But then, when I added one more white rod, giving me eleven rows of 10, and asked how many there were, he said, "200."

I said, "Okay, let's quit for today."

Now, Edward's former teachers gave him many hours of special, individual "help" on arithmetic. But their help consisted in trying to get him to learn the recipes for the problems that he was supposed to know how to do. None of them tried to find out, as for years I never did, just what he did know about numbers, what sort of mental model he had of the world of numbers and how they behaved. As a matter of fact, this boy, if he is feeling good, can carry out correctly quite a number of arithmetic recipes; he is by no means the worst in the class in this respect. But this knowledge is apparent, not real.

The distinction is vital, yet many teachers do not seem to know that it exists. They think, if a child doesn't know how to multiply, you show him how, and give him practice and drill. If he still makes mistakes, you show him how again, and give more practice. If after you have done this about a dozen times he still makes mistakes, you assume that he is either unable or unwilling to learn—as one teacher put it, either stupid, lazy, disorganized, or emotionally disturbed.

It's the same old school rule, all the way from our most hopeless inner-city schools to the graduate schools of our most famous universities: when learning happens, the school and teachers take the credit; when it doesn't, the students get the blame. The words change a little, from bad and stupid to "culturally disadvantaged" and "learning disabled." The idea remains the same. Only when the results are good will schools and teachers accept the responsibility for what they do.

We do not consider that a child may be unable to learn because he does not grasp the fundamental nature of the symbols he is working with. If numbers themselves are meaningless, how can multiplication be meaningful? Trying to teach such children to multiply, divide, etc., is like trying to build a ten-story building on a foundation of old cardboard boxes. With the best will in the world, it can't be done. The foundation must be rebuilt first. Children like Edward, and there are many, would not be in the spot they are in if all along the line their teachers had been concerned to build slowly and solidly, instead of trying to make it look as if the children knew all the material that was supposed to be covered.

The other day I asked the class to find a number of pairs of numbers of which the smaller was one fifth of the larger. Edward wrote 1, 5, and then 5, 25. Then he looked at the 1, 5 for a while. It occurred to him to try the system of adding 1 to each number, giving him the pairs 2, 6; 3, 7; 4, 8; and so on. And that is what he wrote down. The original problem was forgotten, had turned into something else. Edward's unsteerable mental wagon had been bumped off course and was now rolling in a new direction.

One reason children like this have trouble checking their work is that checking requires you to look at, and keep in mind, two very different things— what you are doing, and what you meant to do, what you ought to be doing. Edward shifts his focus of attention so slowly that when he has figured out what he was *supposed* to be doing, he has forgotten what he *was* doing, and vice versa. I sometimes imagine him dialing a phone number. He has it written before him. He looks at it, and begins to dial. By the time he has dialed two or three digits, he has forgotten the rest of the number. He looks back at the paper, and reminds himself of the number; but by now he has forgotten what he has already dialed, and must begin again. Maybe Edward doesn't do this with phones, but it is exactly how he does his math. I can often hear him muttering to himself, "Let's see, where was I?"

When I asked for pairs of numbers, one of them half of the other, he wrote: "1 is half of 2; 2 is half of 4; 4 is half of 6; 6 is half of 8." For one third, he wrote: "3 is one third of 6; 1 is one third of 6; 6 is one third of 12; 12 is one third of 18." Then, later: "1 is one fourth of 4; 10 is one fourth of 40; 40 is one fourth of 70; 70 is one fourth of 100; . . ." Or "7 is half of 14; 14 is half of 21; 21 is half of 28; . . ." The only meaningful relationship he can see between two numbers is the additive one. Perhaps the reason is that he relies so heavily on counting, which is an additive operation.

Edward has acquired the habit of acting unintelligently in math class because for years he has not really known what he was doing. This unintelligent behavior has become fixed, and would be hard to change. But remembering Gattegno and those retarded children, I think it might be done. Intelligence can be destroyed; perhaps it can also be rebuilt.

☐ **March 2, 1960**

> This entry shows that I had already learned something from my experiences of February 14.

A child who has really learned something can use it, and does use it. It is connected with reality in his mind, therefore he can make other connections between it and reality when the chance comes. A piece of unreal learning has no hooks on it; it can't be attached to anything, it is of no use to the learner.

Our first-graders are using the rods. They know them by name and by length. They are used to calling the orange rod the 10 rod, a bad habit which we can't break them of. They can count up to 100 or higher. They have been told, and many of them can repeat, the usual school rigmarole about tens, units, and so forth. The other day I thought I would see how many of them grasped and could use the fact that a number like 38 could be represented by three orange (10) rods and a brown (8). One at a time, I asked them, if we started at the edge of their desk, how far across a row of 38 whites would reach. One little girl immediately took out three orange rods and a brown, lined them up, and showed me. Her expression said clearly, "What's so hard about that?" Every other child out of seven or eight, including most of the able children in the class, tried to do it by lining up white rods, usually losing count several times in the process.

This suggests that though the children call the dark green rod 6 they do not fully grasp that it is equivalent to 6 whites—even though they could probably tell you so if you asked them. Six is just a name that the dark green happens to have; it has nothing to do with its size in relation to some other rod. They look at the rods as another kind of numeral, symbols made of colored wood rather than marks on paper. Asked $5 + 4 = ?$, they take the rod named 5 and the rod named 4, put them end to end, and find that they match the rod whose name is 9; but they don't grasp the way in which this kind of operation is the same as the operation of combining a group of 5 and another group of 4 separate objects.

Some second-graders, given problems like $59 + 42 + 35$, got their carrying mixed up and got answers in the 1200's, or higher. They seemed perfectly satisfied. One reason they did not know that 1200 was too big is that they do not know how big 1200 is. We can't expect children to work sensibly with numbers, checking their work against some notion of reality, when we ask them to do calculations involving magnitudes they do not understand. Perhaps we should ask more questions like: How long a row would 38 (or 50, 75, 100, 200, 500, 1000) white rods make, put side by side? How many white rods would be needed to cover given rectangles, a piece of paper, the top of a desk, the floor of a room? How many whites would be needed to fill boxes of various sizes?

The children are willing to accept all kinds of mathematical shorthand if I tell them that I am too lazy to write out things the long way. In the first place, this is true. In the second place, it gives them a chance to make fun of my laziness, and to feel (which is also true) that in accepting my shorthand they are doing me a kind of favor. They do not like to be told that a certain symbol "means" something. This seems arbitrary and mysterious. But if you express a relationship or an operation in terms with which they are familiar, they will soon be perfectly willing to let you use some kind of shorthand to express it. Thus we can go from "Two whites are as long as one red" to "2 whites = 1 red" to "$2 \times w = r$."

After all, men invented mathematical symbols to save the trouble of writing things out the long way, so what I am doing in class is both logically and historically correct. No symbol "means" anything until we decide and agree to let it mean something; so why not let children feel that they are in on this decision?

We make a serious mistake in asking children to perform symbolically operations which they could not perform concretely. A child should be able to find out which has the most whites, a group of 37 or a group of 28, and how many more it has, before he is asked to do a problem like $37 - 28 = ?$, and he should be able to do this latter kind of problem easily before he is given a rule for doing it. So with all the operations of arithmetic. Numerical arithmetic should look to children like a simpler and faster way of doing things that they know how to do already, not a set of mysterious recipes for getting right answers to meaningless questions.

On the whole I still agree with this. Still, today's cheap calculators give us another path through which children can explore numbers and number operations. We could get a very simple calculator, one that adds, subtracts, multiplies, and divides, but not much else, and show children how to use it to "do" certain kinds of problems. Thus, to "do" $3 + 8 = ?$, we would say, "Turn the machine on, push the 3 key, then the + key, then the 8 key, then the = key, and you'll have your answer." To do 4×6, "Push the 4 key, then the $\times$ key, then the 6 key, then the = key, and there's your answer." No explanations at all about what it means. Then leave the children alone. Chances are that quite a lot of them will begin to invent other problems and do them on the machine, in a highly unsystematic way. Doing this, they will collect a lot of random and meaningless data, as when they were first hearing language. But as with language, they will slowly begin to intuit and test ideas about how these numbers and operations work. After a while they will want to know and will figure out how to make the machine do what they want, or how to guess in advance what the machine will do.

In short, they will begin to make their own sense, their own mental models, of at least a part of the world of numbers.

□ **April 16, 1960**

There are sixteen kids in my math class. Four are poor students; one is fair; all the rest are exceptionally bright and able, with a good feel for math. They have all had place value explained to them many times.

The other day I asked, "Suppose I go to the bank with a check for $1437.50, cash it, and ask them to give me as much of the money as possible in ten dollar bills. How many tens will I get?" I wrote the number on the board. After some scrambling around for pencils and scratch paper, answers began to appear. None were correct; most were wildly off. A few kids got the answer on the second or third try; most never got it.

I erased the original number from the board, and wrote $75.00. "How many tens will you get?" Everyone knew. I then wrote $175.00. "Now how many?" This was much harder; a few got it, most did not. After a while, pointing to the digit 7 in 175, I asked, "What does this 7 tell me?" They said it meant that I had 70 dollars, or 7 tens. I wrote it on the board. Then I said, "Now how about this 1?" They all said that it meant that we had a hundred dollars. Nobody said that it meant just as well that we had ten more tens. I said, "How many tens could we get for that hundred?" They all said 10. I pointed out that these 10 tens, plus the 7 they had already told us about, would give us 17 tens. I then wrote our first number—$1437.50—on the board. We considered how many tens were represented by each digit. The 3 told us we had 3 tens; the 4, that we had 40 more; the 1, that we had 100 more, for a total of 143 tens. I drew a circle around the digits 143 in the numeral 1437. By this time everyone was saying, "Oh, yeah, I get it; I see; it's easy; it's cinchy." But I was skeptical, believing no longer in the magic power of "good explanations."

Two days later I wrote on the board $14357.50, and asked how many hundred dollar bills I could get if I cashed a check for that much. Some answers were 43, 17, 107, 142, 604, 34, 13100, and 22. Only one student got the answer the first time. Four more eventually got it, before I worked it on the board. The other eleven were completely stumped. Again, I put the numeral 14357 on the board, and went through digit by digit, showing how many hundreds were represented by each digit, and therefore, how many hundreds were in the entire number. But I doubt that they understand place value any better than they did before.

This lack of understanding makes long division hard, or impossible, for many children. Take the problem 260 divided by 5. We cannot divide two hundreds evenly among five people, so we must change them into something that we can divide. We exchange our two hundreds for 20 tens. We now have 26 tens in all. We divide 25 of these among our five people, giving them five 10's each. We have one 10 left, which we exchange for ten 1's, which we divide among our five people, so that they have five 10's and two 1's apiece. Our way of doing long division depends on this idea of making change, and a child who does not know that this is what he is doing, or why he is doing it, will see long division, as most children do, as a meaningless recipe which will give him endless trouble.

In his very important and very funny book *How to Survive in Your Native Land,* James Herndon has one very revealing chapter called "The Dumb Class." That class, which he taught for a few years, was made up of the dumbest kids in his junior high school, the kids who couldn't and didn't learn anything. And even among these one boy stood out as clearly the dumbest kid in the dumb class, utterly hopeless at any kind of schoolwork.

One day Jim met this boy in a bowling alley. To his utter astonishment he found that the kid had a paying job there, *keeping the official score* for the evening bowling leagues. He sat on a high chair between two lanes, scoring for both of them at once, keeping track of strikes, spares, etc. Jim points out that this job was not some federal program to give dumb kids something to do. The bowling alley had hired and was paying the kid to keep score *because he worked quickly and accurately*—no one in the highly competitive leagues would have stood for mistakes.

So, Jim thought, I'll give this kid problems about bowling in school. He couldn't do them! His answers to problems about scoring in bowling were not only wrong but absurd. The dumb kids might be smart in the world, but as soon as they stepped into the school they became dumb again. It was the school itself, boring, threatening, *cut off from any real experience or serious purpose,* that made them dumb.

☐ June 20, 1960

How can we tell whether children understand something or not? When I was a student, I generally knew when I understood and when I didn't. This had nothing to do with marks; in the last math course I took in college I got a respectable grade, but by the end of the year I realized I didn't have the faintest idea of what the course was about. In Colorado I assumed for a long time that my students knew when they did, or did not, understand something. I was always urging them to tell me when they did not understand, so that with one of my clever "explanations" I could clear up everything. But they never would tell me. I came to know by painful experience that not a child in a hundred knows whether or not he understands something, much less, if he does not, why he does not. The child who knows, we don't have to worry about; he will be an A student. How do we find out when, and what, the others don't understand?

What first comes to mind is some external test. But what kind? By now I have many times seen children crank out right answers to problems without the faintest idea of what they were doing. They are blind recipe-followers. Some can even parrot back my explanations, but again without knowing what they mean. On the other hand, there are many children who are so paralyzed by their fear of tests that they can't show what they do know, while others who understand clearly what they are doing get confused and scared when they try to put it into words.

Part of the answer to the problem may be to give children the kind of tests I used this year, in which there was a mixture of problems. These tend to throw the automatic answer-finding machinery out of gear and to make them do some thinking about what they are doing. It may help, too, to give problems in a form new to them. But what do we do when the result of such tests is to show that hardly any of our pupils understand anything of what we have been trying to teach them during the year?

It may help to have in our minds a picture of what we mean by understanding. I feel I understand something if I can do some, at least, of the following: (1) state it in my own words; (2) give examples of it; (3) recognize it in various guises and circumstances; (4) see connections between it and other facts or ideas; (5) make use of it in various ways; (6) foresee some of its consequences; (7) state its opposite or converse. This list is only a beginning; but it may help us in the future to find out what our students really know as opposed to what they can give the appearance of knowing, their *real learning* as opposed to their *apparent learning*.

There are many, of course, who say that this distinction does not exist. It's their handy way of solving the knotty problem of understanding; just say there is no such thing. Apparently this view is currently in fashion among psychologists. According to many of them, if you can say that $7 \times 8 = 56$, you know all there is to know about that particular fact, and you know as much about it as anyone else who can say it. The mathematician, the third-grader, and, presumably, a well-trained parrot, would all have an equal and identical understanding of this fact. The only difference between the mathematician and the child is that the mathematician carries around in his head many more such facts. So to make children into mathematicians all we have to do is train them, condition them, until they can say many such facts. Teach them to say everything that Einstein knew, and hey, presto! another Einstein!

It's amazing what nonsense people will believe.

Of course, this notion fits neatly into behaviorism, which is also still very much in fashion, despite all it cannot explain. It is also comforting to teachers, who have felt all along that their job is to drop, or push, one at a time, little bits of information into those largely empty minds that are moving slowly before them down the academic assembly line. And finally, it has set into motion the apparently endless gravy train of programmed instruction and machine teaching, onto which everyone and his brother seem to be happily clambering.

But pieces of information like $7 \times 8 = 56$ are not isolated facts. They are parts of the landscape, the territory of numbers, and that person knows them best who sees most clearly how they fit into the landscape and all the other parts of it. The mathematician knows, among many other things, that $7 \times 8 = 56$ is an illustration of the fact that products of even integers are even; that 7×8 is the same as 14×4 or 28×2 or 56×1; that only these pairs of positive integers will give 56 as a product; that 7×8 is $(8 \times 8) - 8$, or $(7 \times 7) + 7$, or $(15 \times 4) - 4$; and so on. He also knows that $7 \times 8 = 56$ is a way of expressing in symbols a relationship that may take many forms in the world of real objects; thus he knows that a rectangle 8 units long and 7 units wide will have an area of 56 square units. But the child who has learned to say like a parrot, "Seven times eight is fifty-six" knows nothing of its relation either to the real world or to the world of numbers. He has nothing but blind memory to help him. When memory fails, he is perfectly capable of saying that $7 \times 8 = 23$, or that 7×8 is smaller than 7×5, or larger than 7×10. Even when he knows 7×8, he may not know 8×7, he may say it is something quite different. And when he remembers 7×8, he cannot use it. Given a rectangle of 7 cm $\times$ 8 cm, and asked how many 1-sq-cm pieces he would need to cover it, he will over and over again cover the rectangle with square pieces and laboriously count them up, never seeing any connection between his answer and the multiplication tables he has memorized.

Knowledge, learning, understanding, are not linear. They are not little bits of facts lined up in rows or piled up one on top of another. A field of knowledge, whether it be math, English, history, science, music, or whatever, is a territory, and knowing it is not just a matter of knowing all the items in the territory, but of knowing how they relate to, compare with, and fit in with each other. It is the difference between being able to say that a room in your house has so many tables, so many chairs, so many lamps, and being able to close your eyes and see that this chair goes here and that table there. It is the difference between knowing the names of all the streets in a city and being able to get from any place, by any desired route, to any other place.

> I believe this now more strongly than ever, and it seems to me as important as any other idea set forth in this book.

Why do we talk and write about the world and our knowledge of it as if they were linear? Because that is the nature of talk. Words come out in single file, one at a time; there's no other way to talk or write. So in order to talk about it, we cut the real, undivided world into little pieces, and make these into strings of talk, like beads on a necklace. But we must not be fooled; these strings of talk are not what the world is like. Our learning is not real, not complete, not accurate, above all not useful, unless we take these word strings and somehow convert them in our minds into a likeness of the world, a working mental model of the universe as we know it. Only when we have made such a model, and when there is at least a rough correspondence between that model and reality, can it be said of us that we have learned something.

What happens in school is that children take in these word strings and store them, undigested, in their minds, so that they can spit them back out on demand. But these words do not change anything, fit with anything, relate to anything. They are as empty of meaning as parrot speech is to a parrot.

How can we make school a place where real learning goes on, and not just word swallowing?

> I now realize that when we keep trying to find out what our students understand we are more likely than not to destroy whatever understanding they may have. Not until people get very secure in their knowledge and very skillful in talking about it—which rules out almost all young children—is there much point in asking them to talk about what they know, and how they know they know it. The closest we can come to finding out what children really know—and it's not very close—is to watch what they *do* when they are free to do what interests them most.
>
> What we may sometimes be able to do is give students ways in which, if they want, they can test their own understanding, or the correctness of their ideas. But even here we must be careful not to suppose that if one idea for self-testing is good a hundred must be better. The best rules are still the ones that learners make out of their own experience.

☐ September 11, 1960

During a visit, two friends asked me to do some math with their ten-year-old daughter, who was having some trouble. I said okay; the child and I have been friends for many years, and I thought I might be able to find out something about her way of thinking about arithmetic problems. I began with mental arithmetic. I planned to ask her 2 × 76, and when she had given the answer, 2 × 77. I wanted to see whether she would just add 2 to her first answer, or whether she would treat the second problem as if it was brand new. But I was set back when she told me that 2 × 76 was 432.

After some mental calculating, I saw that in doing this problem in her head she had multiplied the 2 by the 6, and then the 7 by the 6; in short, that she had multiplied 6 × 72—correctly, by the way. I asked her to do it again, and again she said 432, showing how strong is our tendency to repeat our own errors, to keep going in the tracks we have already made.

I then said, "What is 2 × 100?" She said, "200." I asked for 2 × 90. 180. 2 × 80? (Pause) 160. 2 × 76? 432. 2 × 70? 140. 2 × 80? 160. 2 × 76? 432. 2 × 100? 200. 2 × 200? 400. 2 × 76? 432 ... Here she stopped, looked at me searchingly, and then said, "Now *wait* a minute." She ran to get pencil and paper, saying, "This doesn't make sense, I'm going to figure this out." On the paper, she worked out that 2 × 76 was 152.

Something very important happened when she said, "Now wait a minute." She was seeing, perhaps for the first time, that we can ask of an answer to a problem, not just "Is it *right*?" or "Is it *wrong*?" but "Is it sensible?" and that we can often see, without yet knowing the right answer, that the answer we have doesn't make any sense, is inconsistent with other things we know to be true.

After a little more work she went to bed, pleased with what she had done. Later, I told her parents about her work, to show the kind of difficulties children get into when they don't know, in general, how numbers behave, and know only unrelated facts and recipes. Her father said he understood more clearly what we were trying to do with Cuisenaire rods; but her mother said, defiantly and angrily, that she couldn't understand all these new ideas, and was going to continue working with her daughter as she had been, by giving her a page of problems to do each day, with the threat that for each problem done wrong she would be given several more problems to do.

This reaction astonishes and rather appalls me. Why should this mother be so eager to have arithmetic applied to her child as a kind of punishment? She reminds me of the many parents I have known who at one time or another have urged me to crack down on their children. Do such people see school as a kind of institutionalized punishment, something unpleasant that we can do to children whether or not they have done anything bad to deserve it? What is it that such people resent so about children?

□ **October 16, 1960**

I asked the new fifth-grade class, "How many white rods would you need to make a row all the way across your desk?" Of the class of fifteen, about half began to use orange (10) rods to measure with. The rest, with one exception, began to line up white rods. When they ran out of whites, they used red (2) rods, but putting them side by side, so that they were, so to speak, acting like whites. When they ran out of reds, they used light greens (3), and so on until they had a row all the way across the desk, which they then counted up.

These children have been using the rods for three weeks or more. They are all accustomed to them, and know the lengths of every rod well enough so that they call them by their lengths. They are used to calling the orange rod the 10 rod. They know it is as long as 10 whites, but they do not transfer this knowledge to a situation in which it would make their work much easier.

I then asked them, "How many whites would you need to cover up one sheet of pad paper [about 9″ × 6″]?" About ten children began covering the entire sheet of paper with rods. A few of these stopped after a while, realizing that every row was the same length. Some of the rest went on to cover the entire paper before finding the length of a row and multiplying by the number of rows. Others, after covering the entire paper, added up, rod by rod, the lengths of all the rods they had used to cover it. Two children began to cover their papers with rods, but they stood the rods on end, so that every rod, whatever its length and color, covered only 1 sq cm. Naturally, they ran out of rods long before the paper was covered; then they didn't know what to do.

Dorothy covered her paper with rods, then told me that 44 whites would be enough to cover it. This was a blind guess. I asked, "How many whites would you need to cover an orange rod?" She said, "Around 8." I said, "Try it and find out." She did, and found that 10 whites would be needed. I then asked how many whites she would need to cover four orange rods. She just stared at me in silence.

☐ October 30, 1960

We did some work the other day on multiplication tables. The results were, to say the least, astonishing. The paper was marked in a grid of 10 × 10 squares, that is, 100 squares arranged in 10 rows, 10 squares in each row. Across the top row, and to the left of the left-hand column, were written the numbers from 1 to 10, but in irregular order. Thus every one of the hundred squares in the grid was in a numbered column and a numbered row. If a square was in the row numbered 2 and the column numbered 3, the child was to put in the square the product of 2 × 3, or 6. The square in the row numbered 5 and the column numbered 7 would therefore be filled with the number 35. And so on.

From Marjorie's paper, I got: 4 × 6 = 22, 4 × 4 = 20, 4 × 7 = 32. Then, 10 × 10 = 20, and right beside it, 10 × 2 = 22. Then, side by side in the row numbered 8, 8 × 8 = 48, 8 × 6 = 59, 8 × 4 = 40, 8 × 7 = 49, 8 × 9 = 42. In the 7 row, 7 × 5 = 35, 7 × 8 = 24, 7 × 7 = 47, 7 × 9 = 45.

I'm not making this up, I swear it!

In the 9 row we have 9 × 9 = 69, 9 × 10 = 40. In the 4 row, 4 × 8 = 62, 4 × 9 = 40.

Is it enough to say of this child that she does not know her tables?

☐ November 12, 1960

A few days ago, when I was working with Marjorie, she stopped what she was doing and said, "Can I ask you something?" I said, "Sure, go ahead." She said that when she was adding on her fingers (embarrassed smile) and was counting 10, 11, 12, 13, and so on, sometimes she held up her thumb when she said 10, index finger for 11, middle finger for 12, and then other times she said 11 when she held up her thumb, 12 for index finger, and so on. But one of these methods always gave her the wrong answer, and she could never be sure which. Would I tell her? I said, "Can you give me an example of the kind of problem that might make you do this?" But she could not. This kind of child seldom can.

What she needs is a broom to sweep out her mind. She has so much junk in there, and her filing systems are in such a mess, that she never can find anything, and the file drawers and old trunks must be emptied out before they can be put into any kind of order. If she could only forget, completely, about nine tenths of the facts and rules she has all mixed up in her head, she might begin to learn something.

The other day I asked the class to find as many verbs as they could that ended in p. Marjorie's face grew panicky as I repeated the instructions. Finally she said, in a near-hysterical voice, "I don't get it." I said, "What don't you get?"—a useless question, but one I can't break myself of asking. She said, as I knew she would, "I just don't get it." I repeated the instructions and asked her to repeat them after me; she did. I then asked if she knew what a verb was. She said she didn't. (She has been given the definition many times.) I gave her some examples of verbs, and she breathed a sigh of relief and went to work. I felt like asking her, "Why didn't you tell me you didn't know what a verb was?" But after some thought, I realized that until I asked her, she did not know herself that she did not know what a verb was. All she knew was that she had been told to start doing something and didn't know what to do. She was wholly incapable of analyzing the instructions, finding out what part of them made sense and what did not, where her knowledge ended and her ignorance began.

Children like Marjorie get in the habit of waiting for teachers to show them how to do everything, so that they may continue by a process of blind imitation; they never learn how to get information out of verbal instructions. In fact, they do not seem to believe that verbal instructions contain information. They do not expect to be able to figure out from mere words what it is that one wants them to do. Nor can they distinguish between the goal and the route needed to get there, the job to be done, and the method needed to do it. If someone gives them a problem, they either know or don't know "how to do it." If they don't, the problem itself is meaningless to them.

And this is the great danger of asking children to manipulate symbols whose concrete meaning they do not understand. After a while they come to feel, like Marjorie, that all symbols are meaningless. Our teaching is too full of words, and they come too soon.

☐ **January 26, 1961**

I have described (pp. 156–160 ff.) the problem that Dr. Gattegno gave to his demonstration class of retarded children. The other day I gave this prob-

lem to Dorothy, certainly the slowest child I have
ever taught. Until now, every child who has tried
the problem has done it in one or two tries; she took
five or six before she said "I see what you're doing."
When she was able to find the correct rod to fill the
empty space, without trial and error or even hesitation, I said, "You're getting too hard to trick," and
switched to another game.

Some teachers would wonder what is the point of
this kind of game. First, and most important, it gives
this child a problem that she can solve, on her own,
without help from outside and without recourse to
formulae, devices, or recipes dimly remembered
and never understood; secondly, it enables her to
grasp a fundamental fact about the way in which
physical objects behave, a fact which, up until now,
she has never grasped, i.e., the behavior of inani-
mate objects is consistent and reliable, rather than
whimsical and unpredictable.

It is easy to feel sometimes that such children
have duller senses. It's as if they do not see what we
see. Once I asked Dorothy to tell me what rod was
the same length as six (or four, or some other number) white rods. Quite often she would take a rod
that was two or three centimeters too long or too
short, and not be sure that it would not fit until she
had carefully put it beside the white rods. Did her
senses send her no message until that moment? Or
is it that she was afraid to trust such messages as her
senses did send?

With enough time, it might be possible to go back
to the beginning and rebuild this child's intelligence. Just as mathematics, improperly used, has

helped to destroy it, so, properly used, it could help to rebuild it. But this could not be done unless the outside world left her alone while she was learning to make sense of things, and did not try to make her appear to know what she did not know, and did not try to make her feel foolish or ashamed for knowing so little. Clearly this is too much to ask.

To "rebuild this child's intelligence" is the wrong phrase, and a bad phrase. We did more than enough harm in school when we thought we were only teaching facts. If the day comes when we think our task is to build or rebuild intelligence, we will do far more harm. Human beings are born intelligent. We are by nature question-asking, answer-making, problem-solving animals, and we are *extremely* good at it, above all when we are little. But under certain conditions, which may exist anywhere and certainly exist almost all of the time in almost all schools, we stop using our greatest intellectual powers, stop wanting to use them, even stop believing that we have them.

The remedy is not to think of more and more tricks for "building intelligence," but to do away with the conditions that make people act stupidly, and instead make available to them a wide variety of situations in which they are likely once again to start acting intelligently. The mind and spirit, like the body, will heal itself of most wounds if we do not keep tearing them open to make sure they are healing.

That class was indeed very valuable to Dorothy. In her first six years of school she had done, according to the school's tests and measurements, about half a year's worth of schoolwork each year. In this class she did a whole year's worth. But it was not because I taught her a lot of wonderful stuff or rebuilt her intelligence. The fact was that I taught her very little, spent very little time working with her; it was not until late winter that I felt she was enough at home and unafraid in the class so that I *could* begin to do some work with her.

What helped her was the fact that, certainly compared with most school classes, our class was a lively, interesting, cooperative, and generally unthreatening place. Freed from her worries about getting into trouble and looking stupid, she was able after a while to come up out of her self-dug hole, look around, and see what was going on. She had not been in the class more than a couple of months when her mother called me one day to thank me for all I had done for her. Since I had spent almost no time working with her, and since her schoolwork remained atrocious, I was not sure what the mother meant. Like my students, I fished for a clue. Her mother told me that for six years Dorothy had come home from school silent, and remained silent all through the evenings. Now, she said, Dorothy gets into the car talking, and talks all the way home and right through the evening. About what? About her gifted teacher, Mr. Holt? Not at all. She talked about all the interesting things that were said and done *by the other children in the class.* That was where she got her food for thought.

Of course, I am happy to give myself some credit for allowing and in some ways helping this to happen. But I was not "rebuilding Dorothy's intelligence," and the most valuable parts of the school day for her were not the hours during which she was working with me.

☐ **January 30, 1961**

I asked Andy to make five piles of white rods, with eight in each pile; any small object would have done as well. Then I gave him eight paper cups, and asked him to divide the white rods evenly among the cups. A child who understood multiplication would have known right away that 5 rods were needed for each cup. A somewhat less able child might have said, "5 $\times$ 8 = 40; I have 40 rods; if I divide them up among 8 cups I will have 5 rods in each cup." Andy did neither. He started by trying to put 8 rods in each cup, ran out of rods, and said, "That won't work." Then he put 4 rods in each cup, which gave him 8 rods left over. I thought he would distribute these among the 8 cups; to my amazement he emptied all the cups and started all over. Then he tried to put 6 rods in each cup; not enough rods. Then he tried 5 rods per cup, which worked.

One of the beauties of this kind of work is that Andy had no idea, as he struggled toward the solution, that he was making mistakes. In his clumsy way he was doing a piece of research, and without having to be told that it was so, he saw that every unsuccessful attempt brought him closer to the answer he sought. What was, for a fifth-grader, a very poor piece of mathematical work, gave him no feeling of failure or shame, but instead a lively satisfaction, something he rarely gets in school.

Ted did some division problems. Given 86 to divide by 2, he had no trouble: 2 into 8 gives 4, 2 into 6 gives 3, so the answer is 43. But when given 96 to divide by 2, he did exactly the same thing: 2 into 9 gives 4, with 1 left over; 2 into 6 gives 3. Again he wrote 43 for the answer. What to do with that leftover 1 he had not the faintest idea. I asked him to divide 55 by 5. His answer was 11. Then 65. Same answer. Then 75. Same answer. Then 85 and 95. Same answer. He was somewhat uneasy about this, because he said defensively, as if justifying himself, "9 divided by 5 is 1, 5 divided by 5 is 1." But he could not get himself out of the jam.

We did some division by distributing rods among paper cups: I gave him 5 orange (10) and 2 white (1) rods, and asked him to divide them evenly among 4 paper cups. Right away he put 1 orange rod in each cup; then he asked me to give him 10 whites in place of the orange rod he had left over. He then distributed his 12 whites among the four cups, and thus got the correct answer—13.

He did a number of problems like this. Each time he had one or more orange rods left over after he had divided them up among the cups, and each time he asked me to change these leftover rods into whites. Now and then, before giving him his change, I would ask him if he could tell how many of these whites each of his paper cups would get. Quite often he could tell me. Thus, dividing 32 by 2, he put an orange rod in each cup, and then told me, after I had asked him, that the remaining 12 white rods could be divided up 6 to a cup, so that each cup would get a total of 16. But when the divisor was larger than 2 he was uneasy when asked this question, and he never asked it of himself. Each time he wanted all his change in whites, which he painstakingly divided up to get his answer.

This is as it should be. When children are doing concrete operations like this, doing things that they feel are sensible, getting answers by themselves, answers that they can be sure are right, there is much to be said for letting them use a cumbersome method until they feel thoroughly secure in it, before suggesting the possibility that there may be an easier way. It is often said that children find security in drill, in repetitive work. In this kind of situation, where the child is in command, master of his materials and sure of what he is doing, the statement is probably correct. But not one percent of school drill is work of this nature. It is mumbo-jumbo, and the notion that if a child repeats a meaningless statement or process enough times it will become meaningful is as absurd as the notion that if a parrot imitates human speech long enough it will know what it is talking about. This very intelligent boy has been drilled many times in the multiplication tables and the approved method of division, and he is worse off now than the first day he heard them. They make no more sense to him than they ever did, and they scare him a lot more. But if he does these operations enough times with rods, or other materials, so that he can begin to do them in his head without rods, if he can get to the point where he does not have to distribute every last white rod before figuring his answer, we may be able to translate some of these operations into symbols that make some sense to him.

Seymour Papert, in *Mindstorms* (Basic Books, 1980), which is about how computers (though *only* if very different from present ones) might be used by children to gain a much clearer insight into their own mathematical thinking, points out the very important difference between "drill" and "practice." Practice you do for yourself, to get better at something you want or need to do. Drill you do for other people, perhaps so they can check up on you to make sure you know what you are supposed to, perhaps only so they can keep you busy.

Was I doing practice or drill with this boy? Mostly drill, I'm afraid. I liked him, and he knew it, and on the whole I think he liked and trusted me. Certainly he was having more fun in this class than he had ever before had in school, and was doing better. But I never saw him doing *by himself* any of these clever things I did with him. And that may well be one of the reasons why none of the things he learned while working with me ever stuck, why we had to go over the same ground day after day, week after week.

What I was doing with him, trying to make things easy for him, was a kind of programmed instruction. As long as I was there to ask the questions, he could in time, with some trial and error, usually figure out how to give me the answers I wanted. But like the eleventh-grader I spoke of, he could never remember the questions. He could (if I went slowly enough) follow me down the trail, *but he could never find the trail himself.* I wanted to give him, for his own use, a way of using the rods to do and check various operations in the world of numbers. But he never internalized, never took possession of any of these ideas. They remained mine.

The whole idea of his learning to do division was mine. He didn't want to learn it, had no use for it—just as I, outside the schoolroom, have *never* had a use for it. It was something he had to do only to please or satisfy me. He may have had a shrewd intuition that if he could *just once* satisfy *me* that he knew how to do division, no one else would ever bother him about it— which would almost certainly have been true.

☐ February 3, 1961

Poor Marjorie has tried her best to remember everything anyone has ever told her in school, without being able to make any sense out of any of it, perhaps without even feeling that there was any sense to be made. For her pains, she has a headful of scrambled facts and recipes, few if any of them available on demand, and no idea in the world which of them may be applicable to any given situation.

The other day she asked if she could work with me and the rods. I said "Sure." First we did the color-rectangle problem: I put some rods together, side by side, to make a rectangle; then I asked her to make a rectangle of the same size, all one color, but using a different color from mine. She saw quickly that it could be done with whites, and soon could do it with other colors as well.

> "I put some rods together . . ." I still think this is a pretty good game or puzzle to do with the rods, if you are using them. The next year I made, out of the cardboard the laundry used to put in shirts (when we sent shirts to a laundry), a number of shallow cardboard boxes, all 1 cm deep, and with different lengths and widths—3 cm × 5 cm, 4 cm × 7 cm, etc. I would give these to children and ask them to fill them up in different ways—rods of one color, rods of many colors, rods of two colors but with the same number of rods of each color, and so on. Young children might find such puzzles quite interesting to do, for many reasons. The people who make the rods might be wise to make, out of molded plastic, an assortment of such boxes. But they're very easy to make out of cardboard or tagboard.

While working she said something that she was to say again many times during the sessions that we worked together—and the written word fails dismally to convey the joy and excitement in her voice—"Oh, this is neat! I love it when you get the trick!"

A day or so later I challenged her to make a rectangle of rods, all one color, such that I could not cover it with a different color (excluding white).

After much trial and error she found that she could defeat me with squares of 3, 5, or 7 cm. From this she concluded that one of 9 cm would do as well, and was surprised when I was able to cover it with light green (3) rods. She did not see that prime numbers were what was needed; but then, though we have been working with prime numbers for weeks, she hasn't a notion of what a prime number is.

Again and again she said how neat it was to get the trick. This is the phrase which she (and not she alone) uses to describe the feeling of having worked something out for yourself and having understood what you did. For all but a few kids in the class, it is an experience so unique that they think of it as having nothing to do with school.

Later we played the division game with paper cups. Like the other children, Marjorie distributed among the cups as many orange and white rods as she could distribute evenly, and then made change with what was left. She liked this game very much, and today had some races with Anna, who is, on the whole, a quicker math student.

These kids would undoubtedly say, if asked, that they were doing division; but they do not think of it that way to themselves, and they do not apply what few division facts they do know. Every time they go through the complicated rigmarole of making change. This suggests that even if we get smart enough to let children do arithmetic operations in the concrete before doing them with symbols—and to get schools and teachers to this point will not be easy—we must still beware of trying to force children into too quick generalizations about what they have been doing. Instead we must find situations in which they will want to find better methods of performing these concrete operations—like the division races between Marjorie and Anna—so that, in the search for better methods, they will make generalizations of their own.

For example, imagine a child who does not know that 42 divided by 3 is 14, and has no recipe for getting the answer. We give him 4 orange and 2 white rods, to divide evenly among 3 cups. He puts an orange rod in each cup, exchanges his remaining orange rod for 10 whites, distributes the 12 whites among the 3 cups, and finds that each cup has 14. He will do this many times before he sees that, when he has that leftover orange and 2 whites to divide among three cups, he can do the rest of the problem in his head without having to go to the trouble of making change.

The other day I thought I could force this process. When a child asked me to change an orange rod into whites, I asked him instead if he could tell me, without actually making the change and using the rods, how many whites each cup would get. If the division factor was one he knew, he could usually tell me; but it never occurred to him to do it when I did not ask the question. Left alone, he went back to his old system, in which he felt that he knew what he was doing.

We cannot overestimate the importance of this. The idea of doing the dividing mentally rather than with white rods did not stick in the minds of these children because it was my idea, not theirs; there was no place for it in their minds; it did not meet any felt intellectual need. We must not fool ourselves, as for years I fooled myself, into thinking that guiding children to answers by carefully chosen leading questions is in any important respect different from just telling them the answers in the first place. Children who have been led up to answers by teachers' questions are later helpless unless they can remember the questions, or ask themselves similar questions, and this is exactly what they cannot do. The only answer that really sticks in a child's mind is the answer to a question that he asked or might ask of himself.

Yesterday we played a different game. I gave Marjorie 2 white rods, and asked how many differently shaped rectangles she could make by putting them together. She saw that there was only one. I added a rod, making 3 rods, and asked her again. Again, only one way to make it. With 4 rods, there were two possible rectangles, a 1×4 and a 2×2. And so we worked our way up to 20, finding the factors of each number along the way, and noting which numbers were prime. At no time on the way up to 20 did it occur to Marjorie, or the generally more able Anna, that they could solve the problem by making use of what little they knew about factors. Given 10 rods, they did not think, "We can make a rectangle 5 rods long and 2 wide"; they had to work by trial and error each time. But they did get progressively quicker at seeing which combinations were possible and which were not.

I did not see until later that this increased quickness and skill was the beginning, the seed of a generalized understanding. An example comes to mind, that was repeated many times. When the children had 12 rods, they made a 6 × 2 rectangle. Then both of them divided that rectangle in half and put the halves together to make a 4 × 3 rectangle. As they worked, their attack on the problem became more economical and organized. They were a long way from putting their insights and understandings into words, but they were getting there. The essential is that this sort of process not be rushed.

This work has changed most of my ideas about the way to use Cuisenaire rods and other materials. It seemed to me at first that we could use them as devices for packing in recipes much faster than before, and many teachers seem to be using them this way. But this is a great mistake. What we ought to do is use these materials to enable children to make for themselves, out of their own experience and discoveries, a solid and growing understanding of the ways in which numbers and the operations of arithmetic work. Our aim must be to build soundly, and if this means that we must build more slowly, so be it. Some things we will be able to do much earlier than we used to—fractions, for example. Others, like long division, may have to be put off until later. The work of the children themselves will tell us.

As I wrote in issues No. 4 and No. 6 of *Growing Without Schooling,* and have been saying to teachers for four or five years now, *if* we think we have to "teach" children what the schools call "basic arithmetic facts," e.g., that 3 + 4 = 7 and 5 × 4 = 20, a better way to do it is by having them *discover for themselves,* by experiment, as these two girls were doing, some of the basic *properties* of numbers. The statement that $3 + 2 = 5$ is best understood, not as a statement about addition which someone invented and which can be learned only be being memorized, but as a statement about one property of the number 5. This property, that a group of five objects may be split up into a group of three objects and another of two objects, is not a human invention *but a fact of nature*. The statement $3 + 2 = 5$ is only one of several ways to write and talk about this fact of nature.

One of several? The others are $2 + 3 = 5$, $5 - 2 = 3$, and $5 - 3 = 2$. All four of these statements, which the schools usually teach as separate and unconnected facts, to be memorized separately, can and should be understood as different ways of talking about *one* fact, the fact of nature just mentioned, that from a group of five objects we can make a group of three objects and a group of two objects.

But that fact of nature is something that children can discover themselves. They don't have to take it on faith and hang on to it through blind memory. They can use the real world and their own senses to find it out, check it, and find it out again as many times as they have to. However, let me emphasize once again the "if" in "*If* we think we have to teach children these facts . . ." We must *not* assume that if we did not teach these facts no child would ever learn them. Nor should we assume that once we have shown children how they can find this basic property of the number 5 they will then choose to spend much time trying to find the properties of many other numbers. For most children it will not be an interesting task.

What is most important from the point of view of understanding arithmetic is the basic idea that statements like $4 + 3 = 7$ and $9 \times 5 = 45$ are *statements about the real world which we can use the real world to check if and when we want to.* Having once satisfied the children (or ourselves) that this can be done, there is no good reason to spend much time doing it.

☐ March 11, 1961

Dorothy was working with me the other day. I have been trying to get to the bottom of her misunderstanding of numbers so that I might find some solid ground to start building on. I think we may have touched the bottom, but it was a long way down.

On the table I made 2 rows of white rods, 5 in each row. As I made them, I said, "Here are 2 rows, same number of rods in each row." She agreed. I asked how many rods I had used to make these 2 rows. She said 10. I wrote 10 on a piece of paper beside us and put a check beside it. Then I made 2 rows of 7. She agreed that the rows were equal, and told me, when I asked, that I had used 14 rods to make them. She had to count them, of course. I wrote 14 and put a check beside it.

Then I said, "Now you make some." She pushed my rows back into the pile, and then brought out some rods, with which she made 2 rows of 6. I asked how many she had used, and she counted up to 12. I wrote this down and put a check beside it. Then I asked her to see if she could make 2 rows with the same number in each row and no rods left over, using 11 rods. She pushed her 10 rods back into the pile, then counted out 11 rods from the pile and tried to make them into 2 equal rows. After a while she said, "It won't work." I agreed that it wouldn't, wrote down 11, and put a big X beside it.

Then I said, "Some numbers work, like 10 and 14, and others don't, like 11. I'd like you to start with 6, and tell me which numbers work and which ones don't." After what we had been doing, these instructions were clear. She counted out 6 rods, which she made into 2 rows of 3. I wrote down 6 and checked it. Then I got my first surprise. Instead of bringing out one more rod to give herself 7, she pushed all of them back into the pile, then counted out 7 rods, and tried to make 2 equal rows out of them. After a while she said, "It won't work." I wrote 7, with an X beside it. Then she pushed all the rods back into the pile, counted out 8, made 2 rows of 4, and said "8 works." Then she pushed them all back, counted out 9, could not make 2 rows, and told me so. And she followed exactly this procedure all the way up to about 14.

Then she made a big step. Having done 14, she brought out another rod to make 15, and merely added that rod to one of the rows, before telling me that 15 would not work. Again she left her rows, this time adding another rod to the short row, before telling me that 16 would work. This more efficient process she continued up into the early 20's—about 24, I think. Then, having found that 24 would work, she said, but without using the rods, "25 won't work." I wrote it, and she continued thus, with increasing speed and confidence, until we got to about 36. At this point she stopped naming the odd numbers altogether, saying only "36 works, 38 works, 40 works ..." and so on up into the 50's, where we stopped.

We rested a bit, fooled around with the rods, did a little building with them, and then went on to the next problem. This time I made 3 equal rows, and asked her to find what numbers, beginning with 6, would work for this problem. To my surprise, she could not arrange 6 rods in 3 equal rows, arranging them instead in a 3-2-1 pattern. I helped her out, and she began to work. From the start she moved one step ahead of where she had been on the 2-row problem. When I had made 6 rods into 3 rows of 2, and had written that 6 worked, she added a rod to one of the rows, told me that 7 would not work, added a rod to another row, told me that 8 would not work, added a rod to another row, and told me that 9 would work. In this way we worked our way up to about 15 or 18. Here she stopped using the rods, and said, "19 doesn't work, 20 doesn't work, 21 works ..." and so on. When she got up to about 27, she just gave me the numbers that worked—30, 33, 36, 39.

In the 4-row problem we began with 8 rods. She used the rods to tell me that 9, 10, and 11 would not work, and that 12 would. Without the rods, she told me that 13, 14, and 15 would not work, and that 16 would; from there she began counting by fours—20, 24, 28, 32, etc. In the 5-row problem we began with 10 rods, and after using the rods to get to 15 she went on from there counting by fives.

People to whom I have described this child's work have found it all but impossible to believe. They could not imagine that even the most wildly unsuccessful student could have so little mathematical insight, or would use such laborious and inefficient methods to solve so simple a problem. The fact remains that this is what the child did. There is no use in we teachers telling ourselves that such children *ought* to know more, *ought* to understand better, *ought* to be able to work more efficiently; the facts are what count. The reason this poor child has learned hardly anything in six years of school is that no one ever began where she *was;* just as the reason she was able to make such extraordinary gains in efficiency and understanding during this session is that, beginning where she was, she was learning genuinely and on her own.

Though I have many reservations today about much of the work I did with my fifth-grade classes, I am still very pleased with this day's work with Dorothy. I don't think that she, any more than Ted, was internalizing, taking possession of, making her own, much of what I was showing her. But at least she was having the experience of solving problems that she understood, and knowing from the evidence of her senses that she had solved them. At least she was feeling some of the power of her own mind. The problem, *my* problem, probably seemed pointless and ridiculous to her, but the solution was hers.

I think it would be foolish, a waste of time,

and often harmful to ask all young children to do these tasks, take them through these procedures. But they might be very useful in helping people (children or adults) for whom even simple arithmetic has always been a terrifying mystery, to make some sense out of it, and more important, to realize that even when we can't for the moment see the sense of it, mathematics is basically sensible.

I suspect that adults who have always had trouble with basic arithmetic and feel afraid of it might find that if they did for themselves some of the exercises described here, they might soon see some of the sense in arithmetic and feel a lot better. Like Marjorie, they might find that they too "love it when they get the trick."

No need to use anything as expensive as Cuisenaire rods to do such work. Any small objects would do—matches (used), toothpicks, bits of paper or cardboard.

☐ March 20, 1961

A number of the children have worked on a problem that could be stated thus: "Find what numbers of squares can be arranged in a rectangle that is more than one square in width." Clearly, every number except the prime numbers will work for this problem. The other day I turned it into a new and more subtle problem by saying that there had to be a hole, the size of one of the squares, in the exact middle of the rectangle. An able student, like

Terry, attacks the problem systematically. He began by trying to make the smallest possible rectangle with a hole in the center, in short, by having just one thickness of squares all around the hole. To do this took 8 squares. Then he considered how this rectangle could grow into a larger one, while keeping the hole in the middle. He soon saw that any such rectangle must have sides with odd lengths—3 × 5, 7 × 3, etc. In another moment he could say, in general, and without any further construction, which numbers would work and which would not.

A slow student, like Andy, will attack the problem in an entirely different way. He took 16 rods, made a 4 × 4 square, and then spent a long time trying to remove one rod so that the hole would be in the middle, but no matter how he shuffled the rods around, the hole was always in the wrong place. It was fun to watch him struggle with this; his failure to get that hole to go where he wanted exasperated him, but—what is unusual for him—it did not frighten him. He was working boldly and determinedly. Eventually, he saw that he would have to have a rectangle of odd dimensions before the problem would work. Even then, he did not see that any such rectangle would do. Compared with the way Terry tackled the problem, his method could be called clumsy and inefficient; but the vital point is that it was his method, exactly suited to his own store of mathematical learning and insight; and because it was his own, he was learning from it.

With thought, practice, and luck we should be able to devise problems that children can do in ways which, being their own, will be of use to them. Such problems could make up a kind of self-adjusting learning-machine, in which the child himself makes the program harder as he becomes more skillful. But this approach to mathematical learning, and other kinds as well, will require teachers to stop thinking of *the* way or *the best* way to solve problems. We must recognize that children who are dealing with a problem in a very primitive, experimental, and inefficient level, are making discoveries that are just as good, just as exciting, just as worthy of interest and encouragement, as the more sophisticated discoveries made by more advanced students. When Dorothy discovers, after long painful effort, that every other number can be divided into 2 equal rows, that every third number can be divided into 3 equal rows, she has made just as great an intellectual leap as those children who, without being told, discovered for themselves some of the laws of exponents.

In other words, the invention of the wheel was as big a step forward as the invention of the airplane—bigger, in fact. We teachers will have to learn to recognize when our students are, mathematically speaking, inventing wheels and when they are inventing airplanes; and we will have to learn to be as genuinely excited and pleased by wheel inventors as by airplane inventors. Above all, we will have to avoid the difficult temptation of showing slow students the wheel so that they may more quickly get to work on the airplanes. In mathematics certainly, and very probably in all subjects, knowledge which is not genuinely discovered by children will very likely prove useless and will be soon forgotten.

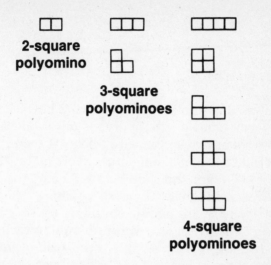

**2-square
polyomino**

**3-square
polyominoes**

**4-square
polyominoes**

These puzzles or problems, about making rectangles, or rectangles with holes in the middle, were quite interesting to the children—interesting, at least, as schoolwork goes. I doubt very much that any of them ever did, or that any children ever would, spend much of their own time doing such puzzles. But for a school class they were not too bad. And like some of the other activities I have described they might be interesting and useful to some math-fearing children or adults.

Some very important mathematical work has grown out of equally humble beginnings, like the study of polyominoes—shapes you can make by putting squares together. (See examples.)

Of course, to work on polyominoes, or the kinds of puzzles I gave my class, you don't need

Cuisenaire rods—squares cut out of paper or cardboard will do as well.

☐ **May 6, 1961**

A very skillful public relations job has been done for the so-called new math. Everyone talks about it, and any school or teacher who isn't doing it seems hopelessly old-fashioned. Some of this new math is really very good. Here and there, truly revolutionary and constructive changes in math teaching are being made; children are finding out things for themselves instead of being told answers or hinted toward them with leading questions. But these places are few. Most of the new math is just what the bad old math was—cookbookery. The difference is that the cookbooks are newer, more up to date—which may be a good thing, if cookbookery is what you want. Some of the cookbooks are not only newer, but better; but many, including some of the most highly touted, lavishly financed, and widely used, are not. Some I have examined are unclearly written; they contain many ambiguities; their examples are often ill chosen; they assume understandings that many children don't have; they do not make sufficiently strong the bridge between the known and real and the unknown and symbolic; they have too much material in them; they are too disconnected, too linear, too answer-directed. They are, in short, not worth all the fuss that is being made over them, and some of the children I know who are using them are as confused, baffled, and frightened as ever.

Seymour Papert, professor of mathematics and of education at MIT, in *Mindstorms,* has this to say about the new math:

> The New Math curriculum reform of the sixties made some attempt to change the content of school math. But it could not go very far. It was stuck with having to do sums, albeit different sums. The fact that the new sums dealt with sets instead of numbers, or arithmetic in base two instead of base ten made little difference. Moreover, the math reform did not provide a challenge to the inventiveness of creative mathematicians and so never acquired the sparkle of excitement that marks the product of new thought. The name itself—"New Math"—was a misnomer. There was very little new about its mathematical content: It did not come from a process of invention of children's mathematics but from a process of trivialization of mathematician's mathematics.

But even if the new math had been good, and a few little bits of it were, it would never have made any fundamental changes in the way math was taught in school as long as teachers were told, as they were, that they had to do new math in their classes whether they liked it or not. The only way to get new ideas and ways of teaching into classrooms is to say to teachers, "Here is an idea we think you might like, and if—and only if—you do, you might think about using some of it in your work with the children." It was exactly in this spirit that Bill Hull and I were introduced to the Cuisenaire rods. Nobody at the school told us to use them, or even to look into them. It was our idea to go to a meeting where Gattegno talked about them; and it was our idea to order some for our classes and try to figure out good ways to use them.

This is the only kind of educational research that will ever actually improve education—research done *by teachers,* in their own classrooms, to solve what *they* see as their own problems. As things stand, many teachers who try to do such research and use the results in their teaching get into trouble—*even when their new methods get better results.* There is no way to compel teachers to do such research, and indeed for some time to come the majority of teachers will not want to do it, preferring to have others tell them what to do and so take the responsibility if it fails. But those teachers who want to use their own classrooms to find better ways of teaching, as I did, should have every possible encouragement. None of the three schools in which I worked after 1958 gave me much encouragement or support in my efforts to find better ways of teaching, even when the results were demonstrably good and in some cases strikingly so.

Children cannot learn much from cookbooks, even the best cookbooks. A child learns, at any moment, not by using the procedure that seems best to us, but the one that seems best to *him;* by fitting into his structure of ideas and relationships, his mental model of reality, not the piece we think comes next, but the one he thinks comes next. This is hard for teachers to learn, and hardest of all for the skillful and articulate, the kind often called "gifted." The more aware we are of the structural nature of our own ideas, the more we are tempted to try to transplant this structure whole into the minds of children. But it cannot be done. They must do this structuring and building for themselves. I may see that fact A and fact B are connected by a relationship C, but I can't make this connection for a child by talking about it. He may remember the facts and what I said about the relationship between them, but he is very likely to turn my words into three facts, A, B, and C, none of them connected to any other.

For example, consider that $2 \times 9 = 18$ and $2 \times 10 = 20$. Most children, and many teachers, see these as unrelated facts; schools and textbooks are used to talking about the 100 facts of multiplication. But these facts are joined by the relationship that ten 2's must be 2 more than nine 2's. Knowing this, I know that 1000×2 must be 2 more than 999×2, and thus I know, without having to multiply, that 999×2 must equal $2000 - 2$, or 1998. But I have found, over and over again, when I tried to point out this relationship to students, that many of them took it in, if at all, only as a third, rather complicated fact, that had nothing to do with the others. A child must discover for himself that if, for example, $2 \times 75 = 150$, then 2×74 must equal $150 - 2$, or 148. Until he does, no amount of talk will enable him to make that step, far less make use of this understanding to see that since $3 \times 50 = 150$, 3×49 must equal $150 - 3$, or 147.

It has seemed to me for a long time that, though children are very good at inductive reasoning, at making generalizations from specific cases, they are poor at deductive reasoning, since even the best students can rarely give examples of any generalizations they happen to know. But the reason children can use so few of the generalizations they hear in school is that these generalizations are not theirs, and were never connected to reality in the first place. The kind of concrete math problems I have been describing gave children the chance to make generalizations, which though crude were really their own, and therefore usable—a foundation on which they could build. But it was hard at first to see how to apply these problems, which I had used for diagnostic purposes, to the task of teaching that conventional arithmetic curriculum—numbers and operations with them. Then I saw the work of Professor Z. P. Dienes, a British mathematician and teacher, then working at Harvard, and new possibilities began to open up.

Professor Dienes has developed a way of teaching math that he calls the Math Laboratory. It was first used widely in the schools of Leicestershire and has been used since then in many other places.

Children are given various kinds of materials, and a variety of experiments to make with them: to find how many of one piece are needed to make another, or how to use pieces of one shape to make another shape, and so forth. No one tells them how to do these things; they figure it out for themselves. If an experiment is too hard, they try an easier one. As they get their answers, they write them down. In time, they start to see that what they do at one time is rather like what they did at another. They begin to see similarities and make generalizations until, eventually, they can do certain problems without having to use the materials at all. Then they can be said to know the principle embodied in the problem.

These materials and experiments are most varied and ingenious. Children find them so interesting and such fun to work that, in the Leicestershire schools, one can often see a roomful of forty young children, even as young as seven years old, working intently each on his own experiment, sometimes with no teacher in the room at all. Some of these materials enable children to learn what few children know here—the meaning and use of base and place in a positional numeral system (ours is such a system, with a base of 10). Other Math Lab materials deal with quite different matters, including some that would be considered by most people much too difficult for the very children who have worked them with ease and pleasure.

There is no reason why, using these materials, the Cuisenaire rods, and other aids that mathematicians and ingenious teachers can invent, we could not teach all of arithmetic, and many other things besides, by the laboratory method. It will take time to find out what sort of materials are most interesting to children, and carry the most mathematical meaning; what sort of experiments can be done by children with the greatest pleasure and with the least possible instruction, interference, and correction by the teacher. But such matters of detail and practice can easily be worked out by schools or teachers who understand the general method and the principles behind it—who are more interested in having children learn something real than in having them get good marks on tests. In such schools, math might, in time, become one of the most popular and constructive courses instead of the most hated and harmful, a source of real and useful rather than apparent learning, a nourisher of thought and intelligence rather than a destroyer of them.

As you can see, I was very excited about the idea of the Math Laboratory, about some of Dienes's own materials, and about the possibility that if we put the right materials in front of children and suggested things to do with them, the children might not only learn but love math. In other words, I hoped we might do with such materials what Seymour Papert in *Mindstorms* believes and hopes we may someday do with a certain kind of computers.

One of the things the British public elementary schools and later our own were most eager to have children learn was the meaning of base and place in our numeral system. They felt that if children really understood these, they would not only not make a lot of the ridiculous mistakes that many of them make in arithmetic, but would see the logic of, and so remember, all the operations in the school math curriculum.

To help them learn this, Dienes invented and had manufactured what he called multi-based blocks. Sets of these were available for bases 2, 3, 4, 5, and 10. A single set for the base 10 contained a number of unit cubes, little wooden cubes, ⅜″ on a side; a number of wooden strips, ⅜″ wide and ten times that long, representing the number 10; a number of wooden squares, ⅜″ high and ten times that long on each side; and some wooden cubes, representing the number 1000, which were 10 units long on each side.

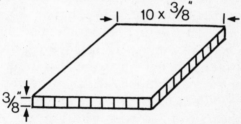

A set for the base 2 contained unit cubes, again ⅜″ on a side; strips 2 units long; squares 1 unit high and 2 units on a side; and cubes 2 units on each side. And so for the other bases, 3, 4, and 5.

The idea was that the children would do "experiments," which were in fact arithmetic problems, but that they would use these concrete materials to figure out and check their own answers. In short, they would learn from the materials. Very excited by the possibilities of this, I ordered multi-based blocks (which I paid for myself) and the experiment cards that went with them. When they finally arrived I put them out in the classroom, told the students about the experiment cards, and said that they could decide for themselves which experiments they wanted to do.

On the whole, at least at first, the children seemed to like these new gadgets, and I waited for all this good independent math learning to begin. In no time at all I got a rude shock. When I looked at the first "experiment results"—i.e., answers—I saw that with few exceptions these answers were not only wrong but absurd. These expensive and supposedly self-teaching materials had in fact taught them nothing. I was right back where I had been with Edward, Dorothy, and the others.

Nor were the children interested for very long in doing these experiments. They were a good deal less interesting than the puzzles and problems I had invented for them to do—which isn't saying much.

I waited awhile for things to improve, thought that if the children used the multi-based blocks for a while they would learn better how to learn from them. But nothing improved. Children who already understood base and place, even if only intuitively, could see the connections between written numerals and operations with numerals and these blocks. Children who could convert 101 in base 2, or 322 in base 4, or whatever, to the equivalent number in base 10, *without using blocks,* could use the blocks to do the same thing, or to verify their answer. But children who could not do these problems without the blocks didn't have a clue about how to do them with the blocks.

Thus, children who already knew that the base 2 cube was equivalent to 8 units, or the base 4 cube to 64 units, etc., could easily verify for themselves that this was so. But the children for whom this was not obvious were perfectly willing to say that the base 4 cube had 211 units or 83 units or any other absurd number that might pop into their minds. They found the blocks, as Edward had found the Cuisenaire rods, as abstract, as disconnected from reality, mysterious, arbitrary, and capricious as the numbers that these blocks were supposed to bring to life.

So I decided to retire the multi-based blocks. This was easy to do. When I stopped urging the children to use the blocks, they soon stopped using them. I left them in the room, where any who wanted to could get hold of them, but no one did. Luckily, unlike most teachers, *I was free to drop what did not work.* No one was leaning over my shoulder telling me I damn well had to use these materials whether I wanted to or not.

I decided I would develop my own math materials. Bill Hull and I, and many others we knew, were much impressed by what we had learned of the work of the "open" primary schools in Leicestershire. We felt that these changes had come about largely as the result of the county advisors, resource people whose task it was simply to make new ideas and materials *available* to teachers, and to give as much help as they could to any teachers *who asked for it.*

I thought to myself that if I could be a math advisor in a school, I might influence the teaching of math throughout the entire school, instead of just in my own class. I proposed this to the school. The school said okay but that they would pay me only half a salary for this work (about $2000—which of course was worth much more in 1962 than now).

I see now that the school was far less interested in this research than I was, and perhaps also a little relieved to get me out of a regular classroom. A year later they were to tell me that, yes, I could still do this research in the school, but that I would have to raise the money for it myself, they couldn't pay me anything. For a year I worked for nothing—there was no money, then or now, to support the kind of small-scale, in-place research I was doing. After that year, needing a paycheck, I asked for my old fifth-grade job back and was told that I couldn't have it.

But even if the school had been willing to pay for it, I think the idea of trying to be an advisor or resource person for the school was a mistake. It was not clever materials, or puzzles, or teaching ideas that had made my class a better place for the children, where they had learned more than they had learned before, but the fact that it was a different kind of human situation. And it was not as an inventor of clever materials that

I was of most use to these children, but as a human being who had done a few interesting things in his life, who had many interests, who loved books, reading, writing, sports, and above all music, who was generally fairly kindly and patient with them but who could now and then get very angry, who did not pretend to be something other than what he was, but generally said what he thought and showed what he felt, and who above all generally liked, enjoyed, trusted, and respected them. Almost any adult who felt and acted that way would have done about as well.

I'm not very enthusiastic about any of these kinds of materials anymore. If I were teaching a class, or teaching children at home, or running a resource center for children, I would be glad to have some Cuisenaire rods around, if someone gave them to me, but if I had to buy them with my own money there are many things I would rather buy first.

What then should we do about making the world of numbers and math accessible, interesting, and understandable to children?

A few good principles to keep in mind: (1) Children do not need to be "taught" in order to learn; they will learn a great deal, and probably learn best, without being taught. (2) Children are enormously interested in our adult world and what we do there. (3) Children learn best when the things they learn are embedded in a context of real life, are part of what George Dennison, in *The Lives of Children*, called "the continuum of experience." (4) Children learn best when their learning is connected with an immediate and serious purpose.

What this means in the field of numbers and math is simply this: the more we can make it possible for children to see how we use numbers, *and to use them as we use them,* the better.

What do we adults do with numbers? We measure things with them, a huge variety of things in the real world around us. Why? So that we can think better about them and make better use of them. We measure, among a host of other reasons, to find out whether we are sick or well; to find out whether we are doing something better than we did before; to find out which of several ways of doing this is better; to find out how strong we have to make things in order to make them stand up; to find out where we are, or where we're going; to find out, if we do a certain thing, what other things are likely to happen as a result. And so on. We don't measure things out of idle curiosity. We measure them *so that we can decide things about them and do things with them.*

Since all this is inherently interesting and important to us, it will also interest children.

So we should introduce children to numbers by giving them or making available to them as many measuring instruments as possible—rulers, measuring tapes (in both feet and meters), scales, watches and stopwatches, thermometers, metronomes, barometers, light meters, decibel meters, scales, and so on. Whatever we measure in our lives and work, we should try to measure so that children can see us doing it, and we should try to make it possible for them to measure the same things, and let them know how we are thinking about the things we have measured.

Children are interested in themselves, their own bodies, their growth, quickness, strength. In *What Do I Do Monday?* I suggested a whole range of experiments that children might do to measure their own size, strength, and speed, and how these things change over time and vary with different conditions. Thus children might measure their own respiration and pulse rate, then exercise violently for a while, then measure their breathing and pulse rate again, then measure it at intervals to see how long it takes it to get down to normal. Or children might do various tests of speed and strength, running timed distances or lifting weights or doing other exercises, and see what happens when they try to do this a second time, and how their performance varies with the amount of rest they have, and how their speed or strength, and their recovery times, vary from week to week or from month to month.

Aside from involving numbers, all this is *true* science, not the passive science of the schools where children are told about the wonderful things that scientists have discovered, or the fake science of other schools where children do "experiments" to find out what is already well known, or to get answers which a teacher marks "right" or "wrong."

Children are interested in money, partly because of what they can do with it in their own lives, partly because of what adults do with it in theirs, and above all, because adults seem to think it is so important. All children of ten and many much younger know that adults think, talk, argue, and worry more about money than almost anything else in their lives.

If I had that fifth-grade class to live with again, I not only would tell them as much as I could about money in the world, but I would tell them everything about the money side of my own life—where I get my money, how I spend it, how I save it, and so on. I would show them financial reports from the companies in which I own a little stock, monthly bank statements from my bank, checkbooks, receipts, bills, tax forms—all much easier to do now, with copying machines everywhere.

Embedded in all of this would be, of course, not only the standard arithmetic curriculum, but much interesting food for thought about social studies, politics, economics, and so on.

If I were teaching children at home, I would put all the information about the family's finances out where all the children could see it. I would let children know that they could take as active a part as they wanted in the financial affairs of the family, including balancing checkbooks, keeping records, writing checks, paying bills, and so on. Many children might take no interest in this work, but many others, I suspect most others, would find it fascinating, and some are doing it already.

In doing this, I would try to put before children some of the basic ideas of double-entry bookkeeping, which now seems to me not only a fascinating and beautiful human invention but, along with typing, one of the most valuable skills a young person can have for living and working in the world.

It might be a fine idea if families kept their financial records as if they were small corporations or business concerns; many children would surely be interested in and would want to take some part, perhaps an important part, in that process.

It would have been perhaps even better if at the school where I taught, as in the Ny Lille Skole (now Fri Skole) I was to visit in Denmark many years later, we could have talked about the finances of the school itself, where and how it got and spent its money, what kinds of records it had to keep and what kinds of decisions it had to make. It would have been better yet if, as at the Ny Lille Skole, the children could have had some part in these decisions.

In any case, I hold to my first point, that the best way to expose children to the world of numbers is to let them see those numbers at work in adult life.

☐HOW SCHOOLS FAIL

☐ February 27, 1958

A few days ago Nell came up to the desk, and looking at me steadily and without speaking, as usual, put on the desk her ink copy of the latest composition. Our rule is that on the ink copy there must be no more than three mistakes per page, or the page must be copied again. I checked her paper, and on the first page found five mistakes. I showed them to her, and told her, as gently as I could, that she had to copy it again, and urged her to be more careful— typical teacher's advice. She looked at me, heaved a sigh, and went back to her desk. She is left-handed, and doesn't manage a pen very well. I could see her frowning with concentration as she worked and struggled. Back she came after a while with the second copy. This time the first page had seven mistakes, and the handwriting was noticeably worse. I told her to copy it again. Another bigger sigh, and she went back to her desk. In time the third copy arrived, looking much worse than the second, and with even more mistakes.

At that point Bill Hull asked me a question, one I should have asked myself, one we ought all to keep asking ourselves: "Where are you trying to get, and are you getting there?"

The question sticks like a burr. In schools—but where isn't it so?—we so easily fall into the same trap: the means to an end becomes an end in itself. I had on my hands this three-mistake rule meant to serve the ends of careful work and neat compositions. By applying it rigidly was I getting more careful work and neater compositions? No; I was getting a child who was so worried about having to recopy her paper that she could not concentrate on doing it, and hence did it worse and worse, and would probably do the next papers badly as well.

We need to ask more often of everything we do in school, "Where are we trying to get, and is this thing we are doing helping us to get there?" Do we do something because we want to help the children and can see that what we are doing is helping them? Or do we do it because it is inexpensive or convenient for school, teachers, administrators? Or because everyone else does it? We must beware of making a virtue of necessity, and cooking up high-sounding educational reasons for doing what is done really for reasons of administrative economy or convenience. The still greater danger is that, having started to do something for good enough reasons, we may go on doing it stubbornly and blindly, as I did that day, unable or unwilling to see that we are doing more harm than good.

When my colleague Bill Hull first came to the school where we taught fifth grade together, he worked as an apprentice to the head of the math department, a much older man who had been teaching math all his life, and at this exclusive school for high-IQ kids for many years. One day, at the end of a day's teaching, he summed up his life's work to Bill in these words: "I teach, but they don't learn."

That's what most teachers know who are honest about their work, and that's what I soon learned when I began teaching in Colorado. I taught, but they didn't learn. A few, good students before I ever saw them, stayed good. The bad students got no better and mostly got worse. If we checked the records of the "best" schools in this country to see how many of their C and D students they were able to turn into A students, the number would surely be pitifully small.

The question I have been trying to answer for many years is, Why *don't* they learn what we teach them? The answer I have come to boils down to this: *Because* we teach them—that is, try to control the contents of their minds.

□ **October 30, 1958**

Everyone around here talks as if, except for a few hopeless characters, these children know most of the math they are supposed to know. It just isn't so. Out of the twenty kids in the class there are at least six who don't even know simple "addition facts" and many more who, whether they know the facts or not, habitually add by counting on their fingers, usually keeping them well out of sight. There are still more who don't understand and can't do multiplication and division. I hate to think what we will find about their understanding of place value.

It would be easy to make up an arithmetic test that without being too long, or unfairly tricky, or covering anything but what these kids are supposed to know, would stump all but a few of the children in fifth grade. Or any grade. The ninth-graders I taught came to me with respectable school records in arithmetic, yet they knew little about division, less about fractions, and next to nothing about decimals.

It begins to look as if the test-examination-marks business is a gigantic racket, the purpose of which is to enable students, teachers, and schools to take part in a joint pretense that the students know everything they are supposed to know, when in fact they know only a small part of it—if any at all. Why do we always announce exams in advance, if not to give students a chance to cram for them? Why do teachers, even in graduate schools, always say quite specifically what the exam will be about, even telling the type of questions that will be given? Because otherwise too many students would flunk. What would happen at Harvard or Yale if a prof gave a surprise test in March on work covered in October? Everyone knows what would happen; that's why they don't do it.

> It is as true now as it was then that no matter what tests show, very little of what is taught in school is learned, very little of what is learned is remembered, and very little of what is remembered is used. The things

we learn, remember, and use are the things we seek out or meet in the daily, serious, nonschool parts of our lives.

☐ **March 20, 1959**

Today Jane did one of those things that, for all her rebellious and annoying behavior in class, make her one of the best and most appealing people, young or old, that I have ever known. I was at the board, trying to explain to her a point on long division, when she said, in self-defense, "But Miss W. [her fourth-grade teacher] told us that we should take the first number ..." Here she saw the smallest shadow of doubt on my face. She knew instantly that I did not approve of this rule, and without so much as a pause she continued, ". . . it wasn't Miss W., it was someone else ..." and then went on talking about long division.

I was touched and very moved. How many adults would have seen what she saw, that what she was saying about Miss W.'s teaching was, in some slight degree, lowering my estimate of Miss W.? Even more to the point, how many adults, given this opportunity to shift the blame for their difficulties onto the absent Miss W., would instead have instantly changed their story to protect her from blame? For all our yammering about loyalty, not one adult in a thousand would have shown the loyalty that this little girl gave to her friend and former teacher. And she scarcely had to think to do it; for her, to defend one's friends from harm, blame, or even criticism was an instinct as natural as breathing.

Teachers and schools tend to mistake good behavior for good character. What they prize above all else is docility, suggestibility; the child who will do what he is told; or even better, the child who will do what is wanted without even having to be told. They value most in children what children least value in themselves. Small wonder that their effort to build character is such a failure; they don't know it when they see it. Jane is a good example. She has been a trial to everyone who has taught her. Even this fairly lenient school finds her barely tolerable; most schools long since would have kicked her out in disgrace. Of the many adults who have known her, probably very few have recognized her extraordinary qualities or appreciated their worth. Asked for an estimate of her character, most of them would probably say that it was bad. Yet, troublesome as she is, I wish that there were more children like her.

Someone called courage "the lovely virtue." It *is* lovely, and nowhere more so than in little children, who are so weak and vulnerable and have so many good reasons to be afraid.

With few exceptions, schools and school people do not value courage in children. Not understanding it, and having very little of it themselves, they fear it, and do all they can to stamp it out. They think that children who are brave will be hard to handle, rebellious, defiant, and that children who are scared will be easy to control. They have it exactly backwards. The defiant, destructive, violent children who fill our schools, in city and country, *are not brave,* and it is because they are not that they will do anything to look good in the eyes of the peer group, the mob of age-mates whose whims and prejudices mean all the world to them.

If the schools could only learn to recognize, to value, and to foster courage in children, a great many of their most serious problems, not just of learning, but also of discipline, would be well on the road toward a solution. But there are few signs that this is about to happen.

☐ April 11, 1959

The things children talk about in class, when they are allowed to talk at all, are seldom close to their hearts. Only once in a great while do I feel, at the end of a class discussion, that I have come close to the real life of these children. One such discussion was about hiding places; another, just a few days ago, was about names.

This latter came up in Roman history. The time arrived in Rome when the mob gained political power, so that the ability to arouse and inflame the mob was a sure key to high office. The kids wanted to know how this was done. I said it was done mostly with names. The way to arouse a mob against your political opponent was to call him names, the kind of names the mob hates most, or can be talked into hating. The mob spirit is weaker in these children than it will be in a few years, and they were skeptical; they wanted to know what kind of names would arouse a mob.

For answer, I asked them, "Well, what kind of

names do you hate to be called?" We were off. Before the end of the period the board was covered with names. About half were what I expected, the usual ten-year-old insults—idiot, stupid, nuthead, fat slob, chicken, dope, scaredy-cat, etc. The rest surprised me. They were all terms of endearment.

It was quite a scene. There were all these bright-faced, lively children, eyes dancing with excitement and enthusiasm, seeing who could most strongly express their collective contempt and disgust for all the names that adults might suppose they like most. Someone would say, "Dearie—ug-g-g-g-gh!" Chorus of agreement. Someone else would say, "Honey—ic-c-c-c-ch!" More agreement. Every imaginable term of affection and endearment came in for its share. Not one was legitimate, not one was accepted. Nobody said of any term, "Well, that's not too bad." To some extent the children may have been carried away by the excitement of the game, but from the way they looked and sounded I felt sure, and do now, that they really meant what they were saying, that their dislike of these terms of endearment was genuine and deeply felt.

Why should this be? Of course, ten is a heroic age for most kids. They remind me in many ways of the Homeric Greeks. They are quarrelsome and combative; they have a strong and touchy sense of honor; they believe that every affront must be repaid, and with interest; they are fiercely loyal to their friends, even though they may change friends often; they have little sense of fair play, and greatly admire cunning and trickery; they are both highly possessive and very generous—no smallest trifle may be taken from them, but they are likely to give anything away if they feel so disposed. Most of the time, they don't feel like little children, and they don't like being talked to as if they were little children.

But there is more to it than this. They suspect and resent these terms of endearment because they have too often heard them used by people who did not mean them. Everyone who deals with children these days has heard the dictum that children need to be loved, must be loved. But even to those who like them most, children are not always a joy and delight to be with. Often they are much like older people, and often they are exasperating and irritating. It is not surprising that there are many adults who do not like children much, if at all. But they feel that they ought to like them, have a duty to like them, and they try to discharge this duty by acting, particularly by talking, as if they liked them. Hence the continual and meaningless use of words like *honey*, *dearie*, etc. Hence, the dreadful, syrupy voice that so many adults use when they speak to children. By the time they are ten, children are fed up with this fake affection, and ready to believe that, most of the time, adults believe and mean very little of what they say.

☐ **May 3, 1959**

The more I see of our troublemaking Jane, and the more I think about her, the clearer it becomes that she has a great need to feel truly loved, but feels that being loved when she is nice, good, obedient, etc., does not count. *Loved* is a tricky word here;

perhaps I should say admired, appreciated, or even honored and respected. She is like Cyrano; she thinks nothing could be more contemptible than to try to get approval and affection from others by saying, doing, and being what they want.

Isn't there much to admire in this? Perhaps someday she will feel that she can oblige and help the people she likes without having to worry about whether she gets anything out of it for herself. Right now, she finds it hard to show her natural affection, as other children might, just by being affectionate. On the contrary, she feels she must continually test, by misbehaving, the affection of others for her. Now and then she miscalculates and draws down on herself a punishment that she thinks is too severe, and so falls into a cycle of angry rebellion that she does not know how to break.

She is at my lunch table these days, and is delightful company; she's even making vague gestures in the direction of better table manners. I wish I could persuade her that she need not every day give our affection for her the acid test, but I guess only time will do that. At lunch the other day she said to me, "I *hate* teachers!" and then gave me a 1/100-second smile and a hard sock on the arm. How much easier her life would be if we did not continually oblige her to choose between our adult approval and her own self-respect.

After school ended, I did not see Jane until midsummer, when I went with friends to a beach in the town where she lived. We came round a corner and there she was, on the opposite side of the street with a couple of her friends. She came running over and planted herself in front of me. "What are *you* doing here?" she said. I said, "Just going to the beach, if that's all right with you." She looked at me a second or two and then said, *"Teachers!"* and something about never being able to get away from them. On that note we parted. But I was very glad to see her.

That fall, since I was teaching at another school, I didn't see her again until about November. One day I was walking down a street in Cambridge and caught sight of her. She saw me and came running toward me. I waited for her to plant herself in front of me and demand to know again what I was doing there. But instead of stopping, she kept on running—and to my utter astonishment, jumped right up into my arms. I was almost overcome with surprise and joy. She knew! In a moment I put her down on the sidewalk, and we stood there awhile, looking at each other with pleasure, but without much to say—how's school, it's okay, how's your new school, it's fine. Then we said good-bye and went our different ways. When I next saw her, she was too old for any such displays of feeling even if she still had the feelings.

Just last summer I saw her again, now a young married woman of thirty-one. I told her that she had been my favorite in that class. She was surprised. The adult had long forgotten what, for an instant at least, the ten-year-old child had known.

☐ **June 3, 1959**

I've corrected and scored the final math tests. The results are not quite as dismal as last week; most people did a little better. But one exception suggests that drill is not always as helpful as most people think. Caroline took the first test after being out two weeks, during which she missed much review work. She surprised me by getting 15 out of 25. Today, after taking the other test a week ago, and after a week of further review, she got only 7 right. It looks as if she learns more when she is out of school than when she is in it.

> This surprised me then; it doesn't surprise me now. Most children learn more, even more schoolwork, when they are out of school than when they are in. As I pointed out in *Teach Your Own*, when children who normally go to school get sick or hurt and can't go, the schools send tutors to their homes so that they won't fall behind in their schoolwork. In most places these tutors see the children from two to three hours a week, in some places less than that. It is enough; the children keep up with their classmates and even go ahead, for now they have time to read all they want, and their reading and other work is not endlessly interrupted by the time-wasting routines of school.

Looking at the low gang, I feel angry and disgusted with myself for having given these tests. The good students didn't need them; the poor students, during this month or more of preparation and review, had most of whatever confidence and common sense they had picked up during the year knocked right out of them. Looking at Monica today, on the edge of tears, unable to bring herself even to try most of the problems, I felt that I had literally done her an injury.

There was a lot of room for improvement in the rather loose classes I was running last fall, but the children were doing some real thinking and learning, and were gaining confidence in their own powers. From a blind *producer* Ben was on his way to being a very solid and imaginative *thinker;* now he has fallen back into recipe-following production strategy of the worst kind. What is this test nonsense, anyway? Do people go through life taking math tests, with other people telling them to hurry? Are we trying to turn out intelligent people, or test takers?

> The answer to that question was not hard to find. What the schools wanted was good test takers. Nothing else was anywhere near as important.
>
> I remember an old chief machinist on an obsolete training submarine in Key West saying bitterly about his worn-out engines, which he had spent many hours polishing up for an official inspection, "They shine, don't they? Who the hell cares if they don't work?"

There must be a way to educate young children so that the great human qualities that we know are in them may be developed. But we'll never do it as long as we are obsessed with tests. At faculty meetings we talk about how to reward the *thinkers* in our classes. Who is kidding whom? No amount of rewards and satisfactions obtained in the small group thinking sessions will make up to Monica for what she felt today, faced by a final test that she knew she couldn't do and was going to fail. Pleasant experiences don't make up for painful ones. No child, once painfully burned, would agree to be burned again, however enticing the reward. For all our talk and good intentions, there is much more stick than carrot in school, and while this remains so, children are going to adopt a strategy aimed above all else at staying out of trouble. How can we foster a joyous, alert, wholehearted participation in life if we build all our schooling around the holiness of getting "right answers"?

□ **March 8, 1960**

The other day a woman said for me, better than I ever could have said it for myself, just what is wrong with the whole school setup. During this past vacation I visited a school that was still in session. It has the reputation of being very "good" and "tough." The headmistress, who was very nice, asked me where I had taught. When I told her, she said with false humility, "I'm afraid you'll find us very old-fashioned." But she made me welcome, and particularly urged me to visit the arithmetic class of her fourth-grade teacher, who had been there for many years and was generally felt to be a jewel among teachers and the pride of the school. I went. Soon after I arrived the class began. The children had done some multiplication problems and, in turn, were reading answers from their marked papers. All went smoothly until, right after a child had read his answer, another child raised his hand. "What is it, Jimmy?" the teacher asked, with just the faintest hint in her voice that this interruption could not be really necessary. "Well, I didn't get that answer," said Jimmy, "I got ..." but before he could say more, the teacher said, "Now, Jimmy, I'm sure we don't want to hear any *wrong* answers." And that was the last word out of Jimmy.

This woman is far ahead of most teachers in intelligence, education, and experience. She is articulate, cultivated, has had a good schooling, and is married to a college professor. And in the twenty years or more that she has been teaching it has apparently never occurred to her that it might be worth taking a moment now and then to hear these unsuccessful Jimmies talk about their wrong answers, on the chance that from their talk she might learn something about their thinking and what was making the answers come out wrong. What makes everyone call her such a good teacher? I suppose it is the ability to manage children effortlessly, which she does. And for all I know, even the Jimmies may think she is a good teacher; it would never occur to them that it was this nice lady's fault that they couldn't understand arithmetic; no, it must be their own fault, for being so stupid.

It took me many painful years to learn just how typical this teacher was.

For that matter, if we took the trouble to look into them, we might find that many "wrong answers" were not wrong at all, but perfectly sensible. A young teacher in Vermont wrote me not long ago that one of the problems in her math textbook said that it took 1½ cans of paint to paint the window trim in a house, and asked how many half cans that was. When one of her students gave the answer "one," she asked him how he got it. He said, "There's *one* full can, and there's *one* half can." Nothing wrong with that; indeed, it's what we would have seen in the real-life situation. But too many teachers, and of course *all* machine-scored tests, would simply have marked this answer wrong.

☐ **April 17, 1960**

Here are first-graders, learning to read by the supposedly well-worked-out and highly regarded Gillingham method. The method requires that they be able to say which letters are vowels and which are consonants. Instead of telling them sensibly that we call a few letters vowels and the others consonants, the method tries to have them learn the difference by definition—always a bad way, even when the definition is good. So the teacher tells them, "A consonant is a cut-off sound, made without using the vocal cords." They will be required to learn this definition, repeat it from memory, and give examples of it. They look confused, but their confusions have just begun, because this definition, though true of many consonants, is not true of many others, like *z*, the *g* of George, *l*, *r*, *m*, *n*, and *v*; and is only half true of still others, like *s*, *f*, *sh*, *ch*, etc. Eventually the children will learn that some letters are called vowels because that is what we decided to call them, but this false definition of consonant is going to give them much trouble in the meantime.

Why do we tell children things that about one minute's thought would tell us are not true? Partly because we ourselves do not need the definition to know what a vowel is, and hence are not troubled by its inconsistency. I know a dog, or a vowel, when I see one, so I don't care how you define them. Also, like many children, we are apt to follow rules blindly, without thinking about them or checking them against fact. But the main reason we are careless about what we say to children is that we think it doesn't make any difference. We underestimate their intellectual ability, the extent to which (at least at first) they think about what they hear, try to make sense out of it, and are baffled, upset, and frightened when they cannot.

Children so taught do very odd things. One boy, quite a good student, was working on the problem "If you have six jugs, and you want to put two thirds of a pint of lemonade into each jug, how much lemonade will you need?" His answer was 18 pints. I said, "How much in each jug?" "Two thirds of a pint." I said, "Is that more or less than a pint?" "Less." I said, "How many jugs are there?" "Six." I said, "But that doesn't make any sense." He shrugged his shoulders and said, "Well, that's the way the system worked out." Precisely. He has long since quit expecting school to make sense. They tell you these facts and rules, and your job is to put them down on paper the way they tell you. Never mind whether they mean anything or not.

That reminds me. In a number of first-grade classes I have seen tacked up on the wall a notice saying, "When two vowels go out walking, the first one does the talking." Very nice. A little further inspection shows that in that sentence there are two pairs of vowels, both of which violate the rule. Now what are children expected to make of this?

> In recent years many teachers have told me that this "rule" is *still* put up on the walls of many first grades.

I told some friends about the lemonade boy, to show why I objected to so much of our teaching. They felt he must be unusual, that most children find school sensible and connected with life. Not ten minutes later, in the backyard, I had this conversation with their daughter, then in second grade.

"How's school these days?"

"Okay."

"What sort of stuff do they teach you?" (I hardly ever ask this question anymore.)

Pause. "Oh, stuff like the difference between 'gone' and 'went.' "

"I see. By the way, can you tell me which is right, 'I have gone to the movies' or 'I have went to the movies.' "

Long thoughtful pause. Then, "I don't know; I can't tell when it isn't written on the board."

We both laughed at this.

Later, swearing them to secrecy (I knew I could trust them), I told the child's parents this story. They said ruefully that they began to see what I meant.

Second-graders, who had supposedly been taught "phonics" by the Gillingham method, were asked by their teacher, "What letter does Potomac begin with?" There was a chorus of guesses—*P, T, V,* and many others—with the children all trying to get clues from each other and the teacher. A few children really knew, and their conviction, as well as their reputation for usually being right in such matters, won over the others, so that after a while they were all saying *P*. And the teacher looked pleased and satisfied! Later, pointing to a map on the wall, she asked, "Which way would you go if you flew east?" Arms waved in all directions, again settling down as everyone got his cue from the successful student and the teacher's encouraging expressions.

Later, in music class, the children were asked to touch their toes when the teacher played a C. The teacher then played a little march, to which the children walked around. Every time she came to a C, she held it. Naturally, the children touched their toes each time. Just as naturally, they touched them if any note other than C was held, and when C was played without being held, they ignored it. And this woman thought she was teaching them C! And she has been doing this now for ten or maybe twenty years—and in one of our "best" schools.

This is typical of schools' thinking in another respect. Teachers, not understanding that children like to learn things, believing that learning is painful (because it is for them), every so often try to make it "fun" by taking some tiny task, in this case recognizing the sound of the C, and making it the center of some elaborate game. Teachers' magazines are full of such suggestions. These games take an enormous amount of time to organize and carry out—and so fill up the school day, bring the class just that much closer to that distant and longed-for closing bell. But they also complicate and confuse the learning situation. In electronics terms, they bury the *signal* (whatever the teacher is trying to get across) in a lot of noise. For the children in this particular class, what was the point of this activity? To march around the room? To touch your toes? To listen to the music? How could they apply their minds to a task when they hardly knew what it was?

Children in the *right-wrong* situation will naturally grasp at every available clue. We teachers have to learn to present problems so that irrelevant clues will not lead so often to correct performance. We must learn to know when our faces and minds are being read, and to mix our signals accordingly. Even more important, we must make children more aware of their own strategies, the ways in which they try to get us to do their thinking for them. I often say to kids, supposedly working on a problem, "Why are you staring at me? The answer isn't going to appear on my forehead." Made aware of what they were doing, they usually laughed. It would be better yet, I suppose, to turn away so that they couldn't see my face at all.

When a child gets right answers by illegitimate means, and gets credit for knowing what he doesn't know, and knows he doesn't know, it does double harm. First he doesn't learn, his confusions are not cleared up; secondly, he comes to believe that a combination of bluffing, guessing, mind reading, snatching at clues, and getting answers from other people is what he is supposed to do at school; that this is what school is all about; that nothing else is possible.

☐ **April 22, 1960**

Trudy had to add $20 + 7$. She counted it out on her fingers. I thought, "What now?" I keep thinking I have plumbed the bottom of these children's ignorance, and I am always wrong. On a fresh sheet of paper I wrote $10 + 3 =$. She counted on her fingers and got 13. I wrote it down. Right under this problem I wrote $10 + 9 =$. When she got 19, I wrote it down. In turn, I gave her $10 + 4$, $10 + 5$, $10 + 3$, $10 + 6$, $10 + 2$. Each time she counted on her fingers to get the answer. Then I gave her $10 + 6$ a second time. She counted on her fingers, said 16, and then looked at the paper for a bit. Then she said, "Mr. Holt, there's always a 1 and then the same number you added." A discovery! I was very pleased and said, "Let's see, yes, you're right." I then gave her more of the same problems, and also $20 + 5$, $20 + 9$, $20 + 6$, $40 + 3$, and so on. She did all of them without counting on her fingers.

After I got over feeling pleased with myself and her, I had second thoughts. Had she really learned anything that she could or would use in other contexts? Did she think it was reasonable that numerals should act this way? Or was it just another mysterious coincidence? Did it make sense, or was it just another recipe, one more thing to remember, one more thing that would trip her up if she forgot it? If she felt that way, she would probably go back to finger counting, which she feels is at least reliable. And go back she did, in less than a week.

I suppose this child has been told a thousand times, maybe two thousand, that when you add a number to 10 you get your answer by writing a 1 and then the number you added, yet when she discovered it the other day it was as if she had never seen it before. What on earth would be the use of my telling her again? When you show a child ten times over how to do something, and he still can't do it, you might as well stop. You're not making any connection with whatever is inside his head. You must go at the matter another way.

One day I asked Trudy to write out her 7 tables. She counted on her fingers to get each answer— even for 7×2. She has been told umpteen times that $7 \times 2 = 14$, and has written it many times. Perhaps she even knows it, in the sense that if I said to her, "What is 7×2?" she could answer, "14." But it is not a piece of knowledge that she dares rely on in a pinch—safer to use those fingers. Counting, she got up to $6 \times 7 = 42$ without a slip. Then she made the kind of mistake that children tend to make when they are bored. She wrote $8 \times 7 = 49$. Naturally, there was no self-checker to say "Whoa, wait a minute, that doesn't look right." Then she wrote $9 \times 7 = 56$; but she made the 6 rather badly, so that it looked like a zero, which is how she read it. This gave her $10 \times 7 = 57$, $11 \times 7 = 64$, $12 \times 7 = 71$. And there was not a flicker of doubt or hesitation as she wrote down these absurdities. She was counting on her fingers, and carefully, wasn't she? So how could she make a mistake?

I took the paper away and asked her to write the 7 table again. This time I got 7, 14, 21, 28, 36, 43, 50, 57, 64, 71, 78, 85.

I took this paper away and asked her to do it again. This time, after a slip that I pointed out and she corrected, she gave me a correct set of answers.

Then I had what seemed at the time like a bright idea. I thought if I could get her to think about what she had written, she would see that some of her answers were more reasonable than others, and thus the beginnings of an error-noticing, nonsense-eliminating device might take root in her mind. I gave her all three papers, and asked her, since they did not agree, to compare her answers, check with a √ those she felt sure were right, with an X those she felt sure were wrong, and with a ? those she wasn't sure of one way or the other.

A moment later I got one of the most unpleasant surprises of my teaching career. She handed me her correct paper, with 7 × 1 marked right, and *all other answers* marked wrong.

This poor child has been defeated and destroyed by school. Years of drill, practice, explanation, and testing—the whole process we call education—have done nothing for her except help to knock her loose from what common sense she might have had to start with. What else has she to show for five years' worth of struggling and suffering over arithmetic? What kind of an adult is she going to grow up to be? How is she ever going to be able to make any sense of the world she will have to live in? What kind of fortresses of delusion and false security is she going to build for herself in her mind?

It is hard not to feel that in every way it would

have been much better for her never to have had to study arithmetic at all. All it has done for her is make school a place of pain and danger, where she is so busy thinking about escape and safety that she can learn almost nothing, and use nothing of what she learns.

Twenty-one years later, it makes me sad and angry to think how little the schools and the general public have learned from stories like this, which could be multiplied by the thousands, or millions, in the classrooms of this country. This child was indeed defeated and destroyed by school. Perhaps not by school alone, perhaps not even by school first. But whatever bad may have happened to her outside of school, school had made a lot worse.

Suppose I had said to her, "Take all the time you want, and do anything you want—all I want is that at the end you can tell me what seven times two is *and feel absolutely sure that you are right.*" Could she have done it? Almost certainly she could not. She didn't have enough trust in numbers, or in the physical world in general, or in herself, or in schools—or for that matter, in me. How could she be sure that, when she had really put herself on the line and said that she was absolutely certain that $7 \times 2 = 14$, I wouldn't come up with some tricky question that would once again prove her wrong and make a fool of her. One thing she had learned in school, and learned well: as Winston Churchill once said, the purpose of teachers' questions is not to find out what you know but to find out—and show to everyone around you—what you don't know. Teachers' questions, like their tests, are *traps*. She had been caught by and fallen into a thousand of these clever traps, and she wasn't going to get caught anymore, not even by me. I might be a little nicer than most of her teachers, might not shout at her when she is wrong, but still, I am a teacher like all the others.

If she had simply been allowed to live and grow in her own way, the chances are good that in a world full of numbers she would have learned more about numbers than she ever learned in school. And even if by the age of ten she had learned nothing whatever about them, which is most unlikely, she would still have been far better off. At least her mind would not have been full of junk—untrue "facts," meaningless and garbled rules, misery, and confusion. At least she would have had a chance of making some sense of numbers if and when she ever had a use for them.

☐ April 27, 1960

We teachers, from primary school through graduate school, all seem to be hard at work at the business of making it look as if our students know more than they really do. Our standing among other teachers, or of our school among other schools, depends on how much our students seem to know; not on how much they really know, or how effectively they can use what they know, or even whether they can use it at all. The more material we can appear to "cover" in our course, or syllabus, or curriculum, the better we look; and the more easily we can show that when they left our class our students knew what they were "supposed" to know, the more easily can we escape blame if and when it later appears (and it usually does) that much of that material they do not know at all.

When I was in my last year at school, we seniors stayed around an extra week to cram for college boards. Our ancient-history teacher told us, on the basis of long experience, that we would do well to prepare ourselves to write for twenty minutes on each of a list of fifteen topics that he gave us. We studied his list. We knew the wisdom of taking that kind of advice; if we had not, we would not have been at that school. When the boards came, we found that his list comfortably covered every one of the eight questions we were asked. So we got credit for knowing a great deal about ancient history, which we did not, he got credit for being a good teacher, which he was not, and the school got credit for being, as it was, a good place to go if you wanted to be sure of getting into a prestige college. The fact was that I knew very little about ancient history; that much of what I thought I knew was misleading or false; that then, and for many years afterwards, I disliked history and thought it pointless and a waste of time; and that two months later I could not have come close to passing the history college boards, or even a much easier test. But who cared?

I have played the game myself. When I began teaching I thought, naïvely, that the purpose of a test was to test, to find out what the students knew about the course. It didn't take me long to find out that if I gave my students surprise tests, covering the whole material of the course to date, almost everyone flunked. This made me look bad, and posed problems for the school. I learned that the only way to get a respectable percentage of decent or even passing grades was to announce tests well in advance, tell in some detail what material they would cover, and hold plenty of advance practice in the kind of questions that would be asked, which is called review. I later learned that teachers do this everywhere. We know that what we are doing is not really honest, but we dare not be the first to stop, and we try to justify or excuse ourselves by saying that, after all, it does no particular harm. But we are wrong; it does great harm.

It does harm, first of all, because it is dishonest and the students know it. My friends and I, breezing through the ancient-history boards, knew very well that a trick was being played on someone, we were not quite sure on whom. Our success on the boards was due, not to our knowledge of ancient history, which was scanty, but to our teacher's skill as a predicter, which was great. Even children much younger than we were learn that what most teachers want and reward are not knowledge and understanding but the appearance of them. The smart and able ones, at least, come to look on school as something of a racket, which it is their job to learn how to beat. And learn they do; they become experts at smelling out the unspoken and often unconscious preferences and prejudices of their teachers, and at taking full advantage of them. My first English teacher at prep school gave us Macaulay's essay on Lord Clive to read, and from his pleasure in reading it aloud I saw that he was a sucker for the periodic sentence, a long complex sentence with the main verb at the end. Thereafter I took care to construct at least one such sentence in every paper I wrote for him, and thus assured myself a good mark in the course.

Not only does the examination racket do harm by making students feel that a search for honest understanding is beside the point; it does further harm by discouraging those few students who go on making that search in spite of everything. The student who will not be satisfied merely to know "right answers" or recipes for getting them will not have an easy time in school, particularly since facts and recipes may be all that his teachers know. They tend to be impatient or even angry with the student who wants to know, not just what happened, but why it happened as it did and not some other way. They rarely have the knowledge to answer such questions, and even more rarely have the time; there is all that material to cover.

In short, our "Tell-'em-and-test-'em" way of teaching leaves most students increasingly confused, aware that their academic success rests on shaky foundations, and convinced that school is mainly a place where you follow meaningless procedures to get meaningless answers to meaningless questions.

☐ **July 10, 1960**

Two arguments are put forward in favor of tests. One is that the threat of the test makes children work harder, and therefore better. The other is that the test tells the teacher how much the children have actually learned. Both arguments are false. To the extent that children really feel threatened by tests, they work worse, not better. And tests do not show what children have learned. Not only do they fail to show how much many able children do know, but they fail to do what one might have expected them to do—expose the child who knows nothing at all.

One day I was working with Trudy and Eleanor, who is, if anything, even a poorer student with even less of an idea about how numbers work. On the board I wrote:

$$256$$
$$+\ \underline{327}$$

I then did the problem, step by step, slowly, doing every step aloud, and giving them plenty of time to think about what I was doing, until I got the answer 583, which I wrote. Then, beside the old problem, I wrote a new one, so that we had on the board

$$
\begin{array}{cc}
256 & 256 \\
+\ \underline{327} & +\ \underline{328} \\
583 &
\end{array}
$$

I said, "We're going to add something to 256 again, but this time, instead of adding 327, we are going to add 328. This time, you do it." Would they see that the answer had to be 1 larger than the first answer, or 584? No; after working together on the problem for a while, on paper, they said tentatively, "353?"

I then wrote a new problem, and did it aloud, step by step, until they were satisfied it was correct. Then right beside it I wrote exactly the same problem, so that we had on the board

$$
\begin{array}{r} 245 \\ + \ 179 \\ \hline 424 \end{array}
\qquad
\begin{array}{r} 245 \\ + \ 179 \\ \hline \end{array}
$$

I asked them to do the second problem. They did not see that it was the same, and bent once more over the paper. After much writing they said, "524."

I did this again, using the problem $88 + 94 = 182$; but this time they saw, though only after some time, that it was the same problem and must have the same answer.

A short time later I wrote $2 \times 12 = 24; 2 \times 13 =$. Eleanor promptly said, "I can't read it that way," but after I had written it the way she was used to, went to work and in time gave me the correct answer, 26. Trudy gave me 68. She read the thoughts on my face and said hastily, "Wait a minute." After a while she wrote 36. I said, "How did you get it?" She went to the board, and wrote $2 \times 12 = 24, 3 \times 12 =$. She did not even notice that she had changed the problem. Then she said, "Well, there'd be one more." Then she wrote $2 + 1 = 3, 4 + 1 = 5$, and then the answer 35, saying "Is that right?"

Not long afterward Eleanor told me that $20 + 10 = 29$.

These children, like almost all children in elementary school, take once or twice every year a series of tests misnamed achievement tests. There are several varieties of these, all very much alike and equally worthless. In theory they enable teachers and schools to measure the "achievement" (what a word to describe what children spend most of their time doing in school!) of their pupils against that of pupils of similar age all over the country. In fact they encourage a kind of cheating; teachers are not supposed to cram children for these tests, but most of them do, particularly in schools that make a fetish of high test scores—which they call "high standards."

The tests are designed so that a child's score comes out as a grade equivalent. The average fifth-grader should score about 5.5 on most of his tests, and such a score would show that a child was about equal in achievement to an average fifth-grader. The confused and hopeless children that I have worked with naturally never test as well as their abler classmates; but they are never much more than a year or two behind. This year, according to the tests, my worst pupils had the mathematical knowledge and skill of an average child entering the fourth grade. In short, they presumably knew addition, subtraction, place value, multiplication, and easy division. But this is utter nonsense. These children know *nothing* about arithmetic; in any *real* sense they don't know what first-graders are supposed to know. An accurate test, if there could be such a thing, a measuring instrument that really measured something, would give them a score of one point something.

No. Much closer to the truth to say that an accurate test, if there had been such a thing, would have given them a *minus* score. After five years of school—in one of the "best" schools—they were much worse off, in terms of arithmetic (and not just arithmetic), than if they had never been in school at all.

How are these high scores achieved? A week or two before the tests, their teachers begin an intensive drilling on all the kinds of problems they will have to do on the test. By the time the test comes along the children are conditioned, like Pavlov's dog; when they see a certain arrangement of numerals and symbols before them, lights begin to flash, wheels begin to turn, and like robots they go through the answer-getting process, or enough of them to get a halfway decent score. Teachers are not supposed to do this; but they all do. So did I. The school asked me to, rather apologetically, knowing my feelings in such matters, but firmly nonetheless; when children pull down bad test scores there is an instant uproar from the parents. And it makes it hard for the kids when the time comes for them to enter their next schools. Schools being what they are, these poor devils are going to have trouble enough as it is; why make it harder for them by making their abysmal ignorance a matter of public record? So I go along with the practice. But is this a sensible way to carry out the education of our children?

☐ December 4, 1960

Some time ago, in an article on race stereotypes, I read something that stuck in my mind but that only recently has seemed to have anything to do with children.

The author spent some time in a German concentration camp during the war. He and his fellow prisoners, trying to save both their lives and something of their human dignity, and to resist, despite their impotence, the demands of their jailers, evolved a kind of camp personality as a way of dealing with them. They adopted an air of amiable dullwittedness, of smiling foolishness, of cooperative and willing incompetence—like the good soldier Schweik. Told to do something, they listened attentively, nodded their heads eagerly, and asked questions that showed they had not understood a word of what had been said. When they could not safely do this any longer, they did as far as possible the opposite of what they had been told to do, or did it, but as badly as they dared. They realized that this did not much impede the German war effort, or even the administration of the camp; but it gave them a way of preserving a small part of their integrity in a hopeless situation.

After the war the author did a good deal of work, in many parts of the world, with subject peoples; but not for some time did he recognize, in the personality of the "good black boy" of many African colonies, or the "good nigger" of the American South, the camp personality adopted during the war by himself and his fellow prisoners. When he first saw the resemblance, he was startled. Did these people, as he had done, put on this personality deliberately? He became convinced that this was true. Subject peoples both appease their rulers and satisfy some part of their desire for human dignity by putting on a mask, by acting much more stupid and incompetent than they really are, by denying their rulers the full use of their intelligence and ability, by declaring their minds and spirits free of their enslaved bodies.

Does not something very close to this happen often in school? Children are subject peoples. School for them is a kind of jail. Do they not, to some extent, escape and frustrate the relentless, insatiable pressure of their elders by withdrawing the most intelligent and creative parts of their minds from the scene? Is this not at least a partial explanation of the extraordinary stupidity that otherwise bright children so often show in school? The stubborn and dogged "I don't get it" with which they meet the instructions and explanations of their teachers—may it not be a statement of resistance as well as one of panic and flight?

I think this is almost certainly so. Whether children do this consciously and deliberately depends on the age and character of the child. Under pressure that they want to resist but don't dare to resist openly, some children may quite deliberately *go stupid;* I have seen it and felt it. Most of them, however, are probably not this aware of what they are doing. They deny their intelligence to their jailers, the teachers, not so much to frustrate them but because they have other and more important uses for it. Freedom to live and to think about life for its own sake is important and even essential to a child. He will give only so much time and thought to what others want him to do; the rest he demands and takes for his own interests, plans, worries, dreams. The result is that he is not all there during most of his hours in school. Whether he is afraid to be there, or just does not want to be there, the result is the same. Fear, boredom, resistance—they all go to make what we call stupid children.

To a very great degree, school is a place where children learn to be stupid. A dismal thought, but hard to escape. Infants are not stupid. Children of one, two, or even three throw the whole of themselves into everything they do. They embrace life, and devour it; it is why they learn so fast and are such good company. Listlessness, boredom, apathy—these all come later. Children come to school *curious;* within a few years most of that curiosity is dead, or at least silent. Open a first or third grade to questions, and you will be deluged; fifth-graders say nothing. They either have no questions or will not ask them. They think, "What's this leading up to? What's the catch?" Last year, thinking that self-consciousness and embarrassment might be silencing the children, I put a question box in the classroom, and said that I would answer any questions they put into it. In four months I got one question—"How long does a bear live?" While I was talking about the life-span of bears and other creatures, one child said impatiently, "Come on, get to the point." The expressions on the children's faces seemed to say, "You've got us here in school; now make us do whatever it is that you want us to do." Curiosity, questions, speculation—these are for outside school, not inside.

Boredom and resistance may cause as much stupidity in school as fear. Give a child the kind of task he gets in school, and whether he is afraid of it, or resists it, or is willing to do it but bored by it, he will do the task with only a small part of his attention, energy, and intelligence. In a word, he will do it stupidly—even if correctly. This soon becomes a habit. He gets used to working at low power, he develops strategies to enable him to get by this way. In time he even starts to think of himself as being stupid, which is what most fifth-graders think of themselves, and to think that his low-power way of coping with school is the only possible way.

It does no good to tell such students to pay attention and think about what they are doing. I can see myself now, in one of my ninth-grade algebra classes in Colorado, looking at one of my flunking students, a boy who had become frozen in his school stupidity, and saying to him in a loud voice, "Think! Think! Think!" Wasted breath; he had forgotten how. The stupid way—timid, unimaginative, defensive, evasive—in which he met and dealt with the problems of algebra were, by that time, the only way he knew of dealing with them. His strategies and expectations were fixed; he couldn't even imagine any others. He really was doing his dreadful best.

We ask children to do for most of a day what few adults are able to do even for an hour. How many of us, attending, say, a lecture that doesn't interest us, can keep our minds from wandering? Hardly any. Not I, certainly. Yet children have far less awareness of and control of their attention than we do. No use to shout at them to pay attention. If we want to get tough enough about it, as many schools do, we can terrorize a class of children into sitting still with their hands folded and their eyes glued on us, or somebody; but their minds will be far away. The attention of children must be lured, caught, and held, like a shy wild animal that must be coaxed with bait to come close. If the situations, the materials, the problems before a child do not interest him, his attention will slip off to what does interest him, and no amount of exhortation or threats will bring it back.

A child is most intelligent when the reality before him arouses in him a high degree of attention, interest, concentration, involvement—in short, when he cares most about what he is doing. This is why we should make schoolrooms and schoolwork as interesting and exciting as possible, not just so that school will be a pleasant place, but so that children in school will act intelligently and get into *the habit* of acting intelligently. The case against boredom in school is the same as the case against fear; it makes children behave stupidly, some on purpose, most because they cannot help it. If this goes on long enough, as it does in school, they forget what it is like to grasp at something, as they once grasped at everything, with all their minds and senses; they forget how to deal positively and aggressively with life and experience, to think and say, "I see it! I get it! I can do it!"

☐ **April 9, 1961**

The section Real Learning described some of the nonsymbolic work that Marjorie did with Cuisenaire rods. But words cannot describe the freedom, the happiness, the lack of tension, the alertness, the concentration, the intellectual power that she showed doing this work. She was like someone I had never seen before. For most of her years in school she has been cheating or bluffing, using illegitimate tactics to pry right answers out of other people, and pretending to know and understand what she did not. Now she was free of the need for all this.

When I hear in my mind her voice saying, "It's such fun when you get the trick," it makes me sad, and angry, and appalled, that in our well-meaning way we have given this child, and many others, so few opportunities for real thought and discovery, honest understanding. We have done to their intelligence what denying them good food would have done to their bodies. We have made them intellectually weak and stunted, and worse, dishonest. No doubt children are clever about fooling their teachers about what they know; but the job is made much easier by the fact that we, their teachers, are so ready, so eager to be fooled, to tell ourselves that children know what a few minutes' careful inspection would show they did not know at all.

☐ **June 15, 1961**

A mother said to me not long ago, "I think you are making a mistake in trying to make schoolwork so interesting for the children. After all, they are going to have to spend most of their lives doing things they don't like, and they might as well get used to it now."

Every so often the curtain of slogans and platitudes behind which most people live opens up for a second, and you get a glimpse of what they really think. This is not the first time a parent has said this to me, but it horrifies me as much as ever. What an extraordinary view of life, from one of the favored citizens of this most favored of all nations! Is life nothing but drudgery, an endless list of dreary duties? Is education nothing but the process of getting children ready to do them? It was as if she had said, "My boy is going to have to spend his life as a slave, so I want you to get him used to the idea, and see to it that when he gets to be a slave, he will be a dutiful and diligent and well-paid one."

It's easy to see how an adult, in a discouraged moment, hemmed in by seemingly pointless and petty duties and responsibilities, might think of life as a kind of slavery. But one would expect that people feeling this way about their own lives would want something better for their children, would say, in effect, "I have somehow missed the chance to put much joy and meaning into my own life; please educate my children so that they will do better."

Well, that's our business, whether parents say it or not.

This woman is attractive, intelligent, fond of her son, and interested in him. Yet she shares with many parents and teachers a belief about her child and children in general which is both profoundly disrespectful and untrue. It is that they never do anything and never will do anything "worthwhile" unless some adult makes them do it. All this woman's stories about herself and her boy have the same plot: at first, he doesn't want to do something; then, she makes him do it; finally, he does it well, and maybe even enjoys it. She never tells me stories about things that her boy does well without being made to, and she seems uninterested and even irritated when I tell her such stories. The only triumphs of his that she savors are those for which she can give herself most of the credit.

Children sense this attitude. They resent it, and they are right to resent it. By what right do we assume that there is nothing good in children except what we put there? This view is condescending and presumptuous. More important, it is untrue, and blinds us to the fact that in our clumsy and ignorant efforts to mold the character of children we probably destroy at least as many good qualities as we develop, do at least as much harm as good.

| No—we do *far more* harm than good.

☐TO SUMMARIZE

When we talk about intelligence, we do not mean the ability to get a good score on a certain kind of test, or even the ability to do well in school; these are at best only indicators of something larger, deeper, and far more important. By intelligence we mean a style of life, a way of behaving in various situations, and particularly in new, strange, and perplexing situations. The true test of intelligence is not how much we know how to do, but how we behave when we don't know what to do.

The intelligent person, young or old, meeting a new situation or problem, opens himself up to it; he tries to take in with mind and senses everything he can about it; he thinks about *it*, instead of about himself or what it might cause to happen to him; he grapples with it boldly, imaginatively, resourcefully, and if not confidently at least hopefully; if he fails to master it, he looks without shame or fear at his mistakes and learns from them. This is intelligence. Clearly its roots lie in a certain feeling about life, and one's self with respect to life. Just as clearly, unintelligence is not what most psychologists seem to suppose, the same thing as intelligence only less of it. It is an entirely different style of behavior, arising out of an entirely different set of attitudes.

Years of watching and comparing bright children and the not bright, or less bright, have shown that they are very different kinds of people. The bright child is curious about life and reality, eager to get in touch with it, embrace it, unite himself with it. There is no wall, no barrier between him and life. The dull child is far less curious, far less interested in what goes on and what is real, more inclined to live in worlds of fantasy. The bright child likes to experiment, to try things out. He lives by the maxim that there is more than one way to skin a cat. If he can't do something one way, he'll try another. The dull child is usually afraid to try at all. It takes a good deal of urging to get him to try even once; if that try fails, he is through.

The bright child is patient. He can tolerate uncertainty and failure, and will keep trying until he gets an answer. When all his experiments fail, he can even admit to himself and others that for the time being he is not going to get an answer. This may annoy him, but he can wait. Very often, he does not want to be told how to do the problem or solve the puzzle he has struggled with, because he does not want to be cheated out of the chance to figure it out for himself in the future. Not so the dull child. He cannot stand uncertainty or failure. To him, an unanswered question is not a challenge or an opportunity but a threat. If he can't find the answer quickly, it must be given to him, and quickly; and he must have answers for everything. Such are the children of whom a second-grade teacher once said, "But my children *like* to have questions for which there is only one answer." They did; and by a mysterious coincidence, so did she.

The bright child is willing to go ahead on the basis of incomplete understanding and information. He will take risks, sail uncharted seas, explore when the landscape is dim, the landmarks few, the light poor. To give only one example, he will often read books he does not understand in the hope that after a while enough understanding will emerge to make it worthwhile to go on. In this spirit some of my fifth-graders tried to read *Moby-Dick*. But the dull child will go ahead only when he thinks he knows exactly where he stands and exactly what is ahead of him. If he does not feel he knows exactly what an experience will be like, and if it will not be exactly like other experiences he already knows, he wants no part of it. For while the bright child feels that the universe is, on the whole, a sensible, reasonable, and trustworthy place, the dull child feels that it is sense-less, unpredictable, and treacherous. He feels that he can never tell what may happen, particularly in a new situation, except that it will probably be bad.

Nobody starts off stupid. You have only to watch babies and infants, and think seriously about what all of them learn and do, to see that, except for the most grossly retarded, they show a style of life, and a desire and ability to learn, that in an older person we might well call genius. Hardly an adult in a thousand, or ten thousand, could in any three years of his life learn as much, grow as much in his under-standing of the world around him, as every infant learns and grows in his first three years. But what happens, as we get older, to this extraordinary ca-pacity for learning and intellectual growth?

What happens is that it is destroyed, and more than by any other one thing, by the process that we misname education—a process that goes on in most homes and schools. We adults destroy most of the intellectual and creative capacity of children by the things we do to them or make them do. We destroy this capacity above all by making them afraid, afraid of not doing what other people want, of not pleasing, of making mistakes, of failing, of being *wrong*. Thus we make them afraid to gamble, afraid to experiment, afraid to try the difficult and the unknown. Even when we do not create children's fears, when they come to us with fears ready-made and built-in, we use these fears as handles to manipulate them and get them to do what we want. Instead of trying to whittle down their fears, we build them up, often to monstrous size. For we like children who are a little afraid of us, docile, deferential children, though not, of course, if they are so obviously afraid that they threaten our image of ourselves as kind, lovable people whom there is no reason to fear. We find ideal the kind of "good" children who are just enough afraid of us to do everything we want, without making us feel that fear of us is what is making them do it.

We destroy the disinterested (I do *not* mean *un*interested) love of learning in children, which is so strong when they are small, by encouraging and compelling them to work for petty and contemptible rewards—gold stars, or papers marked 100 and tacked to the wall, or A's on report cards, or honor rolls, or dean's lists, or Phi Beta Kappa keys—in short, for the ignoble satisfaction of feeling that they are better than someone else. We encourage them to feel that the end and aim of all they do in school is nothing more than to get a good mark on a test, or to impress someone with what they seem to know. We kill, not only their curiosity, but their feeling that it is a good and admirable thing to be curious, so that by the age of ten most of them will not ask questions, and will show a good deal of scorn for the few who do.

In many ways, we break down children's convictions that things make sense, or their hope that things may prove to make sense. We do it, first of all, by breaking up life into arbitrary and disconnected hunks of subject matter, which we then try to "integrate" by such artificial and irrelevant devices as having children sing Swiss folk songs while they are studying the geography of Switzerland, or do arithmetic problems about rail-splitting while they are studying the boyhood of Lincoln. Furthermore, we continually confront them with what is senseless, ambiguous, and contradictory; worse, we do it without knowing that we are doing it, so that, hearing nonsense shoved at them as if it were sense, they come to feel that the source of their confusion lies not in the material but in their own stupidity. Still further, we cut children off from their own common sense and the world of reality by requiring them to play with and shove around words and symbols that have little or no meaning to them. Thus we turn the vast majority of our students into the kind of people for whom all symbols are meaningless; who cannot use symbols as a way of learning about and dealing with reality; who cannot understand written instructions; who, even if they read books, come out knowing no more than when they went in; who may have a few new words rattling around in their heads, but whose mental models of the world remain unchanged and, indeed, impervious to change. The minority, the able and successful students, we are very likely to turn into something different but just as dangerous: the kind of people who can manipulate words and symbols fluently while keeping themselves largely divorced from the reality for which they stand; the kind of people who like to speak in large generalities but grow silent or indignant if someone asks for an example of what they are talking about; the kind of people who, in their discussions of world affairs, coin and use such words as megadeaths and megacorpses, with scarcely a thought to the blood and suffering these words imply.

We encourage children to act stupidly, not only by scaring and confusing them, but by boring them, by filling up their days with dull, repetitive tasks that make little or no claim on their attention or demands on their intelligence. Our hearts leap for joy at the sight of a roomful of children all slogging away at some imposed task, and we are all the more pleased and satisfied if someone tells us that the children don't really like what they are doing. We tell ourselves that this drudgery, this endless busywork, is good preparation for life, and we fear that without it children would be hard to "control." But why must this busywork be so dull? Why not give tasks that are interesting and demanding? Because, in schools where every task must be completed and every answer must be right, if we give children more demanding tasks they will be fearful and will instantly insist that we show them how to do the job. When you have acres of paper to fill up with pencil marks, you have no time to waste on the luxury of thinking. By such means children are firmly established in the habit of using only a small part of their thinking capacity. They feel that school is a place where they must spend most of their time doing dull tasks in a dull way. Before long they are deeply settled in a rut of unintelligent behavior from which most of them could not escape even if they wanted to.

About six or seven years ago I began to stop talking to teachers and would-be teachers about radical changes in schools. Why keep asking them to do what was so obviously beyond their power to do? I began instead to talk about small, inexpensive, and do-able ways in which, without running any risks of being fired, they could improve their teaching of reading, writing, mathematics, "the basics," which have interested me from my very first day as a teacher.

At a teacher's college in Illinois I said that thinking about such apparently tiny and trivial matters as how better to teach children to read or add or spell had made my daily work as a teacher enormously challenging and exciting. I urged them to take this same creative and responsible but also concrete and practical attitude toward their own work. Give up methods that don't work. Keep looking for methods that do. I told them how one of my first students had asked a question about fractions for which I had only been able to find a good answer after thirteen years. Such questions, searches, and discoveries were part of the joy of working as a teacher.

Somewhere in the midst of all this I paused for breath and looked at the faces of the education students before me. They were looking at me intently, but what was that strange expression on their faces? Were they excited? Amused? Puzzled? Skeptical? Angry? No, what I saw was none of these. What then was I seeing? In a flash it came to me. It was fear! Their questions afterwards confirmed this. They did not want to hear about questions waiting thirteen years for an answer. They wanted their answers right now. They wanted to be told what to do, and if it didn't work, they wanted that problem to be taken over by someone else.

Soon after, I met for the first time another phenomenon. At a West Coast teacher's college two young and friendly psychology profs had asked me to talk to a joint meeting of their classes. We met in a small, crowded classroom. I sat on the edge of a table in front, and since I would give my main "education" talk that evening, I talked to these classes about something quite different and altogether noncontroversial—how much food for psychological thought we can find in everyday life. It was a topic I had not spoken on before, and I was exploring the subject and enjoying myself as I talked.

Then I began to notice something. As always, while I talked I looked at my audience, now at this person, now at that one, just a quick glance at each. And I became aware that every time my eyes met the eyes of a student, those eyes dropped. The first two, three, five times, I thought nothing of it. But soon this began to force its way into my consciousness. As I talked I thought, "What in the world is going on here?" I began to pay attention, and soon saw that this phenomenon was consistent; none of the students would let their eyes meet mine. I could tell that when I looked away, they would look up again; all faces remained turned toward me. But the only people with whom I could make eye-to-eye contact were the smiling profs. For an instant I thought about suggesting this to the class as a psychological phenomenon which they might later want to examine. But, thinking this might embarrass them, I decided against it.

Since then I have seen this happen often, though only when I meet with students in fairly small classrooms. Perhaps in larger lecture halls they feel far enough away from me to feel safe, or the hall itself seems to them safer.

Anyway, by now I am so used to these frightened faces and dropping eyes that I am surprised on those rare occasions when I don't see them. I often think, if I could give one piece of advice to these young people with any hope that they might follow it, I would say, "For heaven's sake, stay out of the classroom until you have got over some of your fear of the world. Do something else first. Travel, live in different places, do different kinds of work, have some interesting experiences, get to know and like yourselves a little better, *get that scared expression off your faces!* Or your teaching will be a disaster."

Certainly if I had gone direct from college into teaching, *my* teaching would have been a disaster. Like these young people, at twenty-one I didn't like or trust myself much, and was on the whole afraid of the world around me, above all anything new. Fortunately I did not start teaching until I was thirty. By then I had had three years of experience as a submarine officer, some in combat; I had worked six years in responsible positions in the world government movement, in the course of which I had given about six hundred public lectures; I had lived alone and made myself at home, on very little money, in a number of European cities; I had ridden a bicycle most of the way from Paris to Rome; and, in the course of my work for world government, I had become something like an extra uncle in about fifty families with young children. I had not lost all of my distrust in myself or fear of the world, but I had lost enough so that I could see the trials and failures of the classroom not as threats to my authority or sense of personal worth but only as interesting problems to think about and try to solve.

But what would be the point of urging these poor frightened young people to do the same? They need a job and a paycheck, right now. Schoolteaching is what they have spent their time and money learning how to do. Other than unskilled labor, what else could they do? How would they find the kind of interesting, demanding, and rewarding work that I had had the good luck to find? Perhaps someday intelligent schools of education may help them find such work as a part of their training. None I know of are doing it now.

No, there is no place for them to go but the classroom, and terrified or not, into it they must go. Once there, they will try to deal with their lack of confidence, their weak and fragile sense of self-worth, and their overpowering fear in the only way such people know—*by waging an endless psychological war against the children, to make them even more insecure, anxious, and fearful than they are themselves.*

This war begins very early. A mother told me not long ago that on one of her five-year-old son's first days in kindergarten he began to talk to a friend. Having never in his short life been told that he couldn't talk to people, he didn't know this was a crime. Instead of just telling him her rule, the teacher scolded him loudly in front of the class. Then she made a long red paper "tongue," which she pinned to his shirt, after which she began to make fun of him, calling him Long Tongue and inviting the other children to do the same—an invitation they could hardly refuse. In such ways is the war waged. Not much will be learned while it goes on. There are few signs of any end to it.

School tends to be a dishonest as well as a nervous place. We adults are not often honest with children, least of all in school. We tell them, not what we think, but what we feel they ought to think; or what other people feel or tell us they ought to think. Pressure groups find it easy to weed out of our classrooms, texts, and libraries whatever facts, truths, and ideas they happen to find unpleasant or inconvenient. And we are not even as truthful with children as we could safely be, as the parents, politicians, and pressure groups would let us be. Even in the most noncontroversial areas our teaching, the books, and the textbooks we give children present a dishonest and distorted picture of the world.

The fact is that we do not feel an obligation to be truthful to children. We are like the managers and manipulators of news in Washington, Moscow, London, Peking, and Paris, and all the other capitals of the world. We think it our right and our duty, not to tell the truth, but to say whatever will best serve our cause—in this case, the cause of making children grow up into the kind of people we want them to be, thinking whatever we want them to think. We have only to convince ourselves (and we are very easily convinced) that a lie will be "better" for the children than the truth, and we will lie. We don't always need even that excuse; we often lie only for our own convenience.

Worse yet, we are not honest about ourselves, our own fears, limitations, weaknesses, prejudices, motives. We present ourselves to children as if we were gods, all-knowing, all-powerful, always rational, always just, always right. This is worse than any lie we could tell about ourselves. I have more than once shocked teachers by telling them that when kids ask me a question to which I don't know the answer, I say, "I haven't the faintest idea"; or that when I make a mistake, as I often do, I say, "I goofed again"; or that when I am trying to do something I am no good at, like paint in watercolors or play a clarinet or bugle, I do it in front of them so they can see me struggling with it, and can realize that not all adults are good at everything. If a child asks me to do something that I don't want to do, I tell him that I won't do it because I don't want to do it, instead of giving him a list of "good" reasons sounding as if they had come down from the Supreme Court. Interestingly enough, this rather open way of dealing with children works quite well. If you tell a child that you won't do something because you don't want to, he is very likely to accept that as a fact which he cannot change; if you ask him to stop doing something because it drives you crazy, there is a good chance that, without further talk, he will stop, because he knows what that is like.

We are, above all, dishonest about our feelings, and it is this sense of dishonesty of feeling that makes the atmosphere of so many schools so unpleasant. The people who write books that teachers have to read say over and over again that a teacher must love all the children in a class, all of them equally. If by this they mean that a teacher must do the best he can for every child in a class, that he has an equal responsibility for every child's welfare, an equal concern for his problems, they are right. But when they talk of love they don't mean this; they mean feelings, affection, the kind of pleasure and joy that one person can get from the existence and company of another. And this is not something that can be measured out in little spoonfuls, everyone getting the same amount.

In a discussion of this in a class of teachers, I once said that I liked some of the kids in my class much more than others and that, without saying which ones I liked best, I had told them so. After all, this is something that children know, whatever we tell them; it is futile to lie about it. Naturally, these teachers were horrified. "What a terrible thing to say!" one said. "I love all the children in my class exactly the same." Nonsense; a teacher who says this is lying, to herself or to others, and probably doesn't like any of the children very much. Not that there is anything wrong with that; plenty of adults don't like children, and there is no reason why they should. But the trouble is they feel they should, which makes them feel guilty, which makes them feel resentful, which in turn makes them try to work off their guilt with indulgence and their resentment with subtle cruelties—cruelties of a kind that can be seen in many classrooms. Above all, it makes them put on the phony, syrupy, sickening voice and manner, and the fake smiles and forced, bright laughter that children see so much of in school, and rightly resent and hate.

As we are not honest with them, so we won't let children be honest with us. To begin with, we require them to take part in the fiction that school is a wonderful place and that they love every minute of it. They learn early that not to like school or the teacher is *verboten*, not to be said, not even to be thought. I have known a child, otherwise healthy, happy, and wholly delightful, who at the age of five was being made sick with worry by the fact that she did not like her kindergarten teacher. Robert Heinemann worked for a number of years with remedial students whom ordinary schools were hopelessly unable to deal with. He found that what choked up and froze the minds of these children was above all else the fact that they could not express, they could hardly even acknowledge, the fear, shame, rage, and hatred that school and their teachers had aroused in them. In a situation in which they were and felt free to express these feelings to themselves and others, they were able once again to begin learning. Why can't we say to children what I used to say to fifth-graders who got sore at me, "The law says you have to go to school; it doesn't say you have to like it, and it doesn't say you have to like me either." This might make school more bearable for many children.

Children hear all the time, "Nice people don't say such things." They learn early in life that for unknown reasons they must not talk about a large part of what they think and feel, are most interested in, and worried about. It is a rare child who, anywhere in his growing up, meets even one older person with whom he can talk openly about what most interests him, concerns him, worries him. This is what rich people are buying for their troubled kids when for $25 per hour [*much more now*] they send them to psychiatrists. Here is someone to whom you can speak honestly about whatever is on your mind, without having to worry about his getting mad at you. But do we have to wait until a child is snowed under by his fears and troubles to give him this chance? And do we have to take the time of a highly trained professional to hear what, earlier in his life, that child might have told anybody who was willing to listen sympathetically and honestly? The workers in a project called Streetcorner Research, in Cambridge, Mass., have found that nothing more than the opportunity to talk openly and freely about themselves and their lives, to people who would listen without judging, and who were interested in them as human beings rather than as problems to be solved or disposed of, has totally remade the lives and personalities of a number of confirmed and seemingly hopeless juvenile delinquents. Can't we learn something from this? Can't we clear a space for honesty and openness and self-awareness in the lives of growing children? Do we have to make them wait until they are in a jam before giving them a chance to say what they think?

I soon learned that this, though a problem, was not the major problem—and is not now. Five or so years later, when the supposed liberal, progressive, permissive revolution in the schools was at its height, Charles Silberman and a large team of researchers visited hundreds of school systems all over the country. What they found everywhere was what Silberman in *Crisis in the Classroom* called "appalling incivility" toward children on the part of almost all adults in schools.

Beyond that, there is a vast amount of outright physical brutality against children, mostly young. Adah Maurer, editor of *The Last? Resort*, an anti-corporal punishment magazine, recently made a nationwide survey of schools to find out how many children were formally and officially beaten each year. If the schools that did not reply beat children as much as those who did—and the chances are they beat them more—there were about *one and a half million* of these beatings in a school year. But these beatings, which the schools call "paddlings" though many of them are brutal enough to send their small victims to the hospital, are only the official beatings, done in the principal's office and recorded in a book. How much more unofficial violence may be done to children—slaps, cuffs, pullings of hair, twistings of arms and ears, pinchings of cheeks, slammings against walls, blows with fists, unofficial and unrecorded paddlings in classrooms— there is no way to guess. Surely two or three times as much, perhaps five times, perhaps ten. Verified reports are common of teachers paddling an entire class for the actions of one or two children, or even because the class did poorly in a test. One teacher paddled an entire class on the first day of school, "to show them what to expect."

For every instance of physical brutality, there are many more of mental and spiritual brutality: sarcasm, mockery, insults—what Professor of Education Arthur Pearl, who has spent much time in classrooms himself, calls "ceremonies of humiliation." These begin in the earliest grades, when even the poorest children are trusting, hopeful, and in many cases incapable of doing teachers any physical harm. There are enough examples to fill many books. I have mentioned one; no need to recite others here.

No, the problem is not fake smiles and unmeant praise. It is far more serious than that—a widespread dislike, distrust, and fear of children so intense that it would not be off the mark to call it hatred. Since the roots of these feelings lie in the insecurity, weakness, and fear of the teachers themselves, it is hard to see how they can be quickly or easily changed, especially since they are shared by so many of the general public.

Of course there are some teachers, just as there are some nonteachers, who really like, trust, and respect children. But these seem almost everywhere to be in a minority. Many of them—I have had letters from hundreds—leave the schools after a few years. Some are fired; many more quit. For if you like children, it is painful and soon unbearable to have to spend your working days surrounded by people who don't—and most don't. The evidence for this is of course not statistical. How could it be? Shall we send teachers a poll saying, "Do you hate children?" No, the evidence comes entirely from reports. But I have read and heard so many of these, from students, from parents, from student teachers, from classroom volunteers, above all from teachers themselves, as well as many others who have had long contact with the schools, that I can only assume that what they report is not the exception but the rule. And this violence against children, physical and spiritual, while perhaps not the only cause, is surely a major cause of the violence by children that everywhere fills our schools.

Behind much of what we do in school lie some ideas that could be expressed roughly as follows: (1) Of the vast body of human knowledge, there are certain bits and pieces that can be called essential, that everyone should know; (2) the extent to which a person can be considered educated, qualified to live intelligently in today's world and be a useful member of society, depends on the amount of this essential knowledge that he carries about with him; (3) it is the duty of schools, therefore, to get as much of this essential knowledge as possible into the minds of children. Thus we find ourselves trying to poke certain facts, recipes, and ideas down the gullets of every child in school, whether the morsel interests him or not, and even if there are other things that he is much more interested in learning.

These ideas are absurd and harmful nonsense. We will not begin to have true education or real learning in our schools until we sweep this nonsense out of the way. Schools should be a place where children learn what they most want to know, instead of what we think they ought to know. The child who wants to know something remembers it and uses it once he has it; the child who learns something to please or appease someone else forgets it when the need for pleasing or the danger of not appeasing is past. This is why children quickly forget all but a small part of what they learn in school. It is of no use or interest to them; they do not want, or expect, or even intend to remember it. The only difference between bad and good students in this respect is that the bad students forget right away, while the good students are careful to wait until after the exam. If for no other reason, we could well afford to throw out most of what we teach in school because the children throw out almost all of it anyway.

The notion of a curriculum, an essential body of knowledge, would be absurd even if children remembered everything we "taught" them. We don't and can't agree on what knowledge is essential. The man who has trained himself in some special field of knowledge or competence thinks, naturally, that his specialty should be in the curriculum. The classical scholars want Greek and Latin taught; the historians shout for more history; the mathematicians urge more math and the scientists more science; the modern language experts want all children taught French, or Spanish, or Russian; and so on. Everyone wants to get his specialty into the act, knowing that as the demand for his special knowledge rises, so will the price that he can charge for it. Who wins this struggle and who loses depends not on the real needs of children or even of society, but on who is most skillful in public relations, who has the best educational lobbyists, who best can capitalize on events that have nothing to do with education, like the appearance of Sputnik in the night skies.

The idea of the curriculum would not be valid even if we could agree on what ought to be in it. For knowledge itself changes. Much of what a child learns in school will be found, or thought, before many years, to be untrue. I studied physics at school from a fairly up-to-date text that proclaimed that the fundamental law of physics was the law of conservation of matter—matter is not created or destroyed. I had to scratch that out before I left school. In economics at college I was taught many things that were not true of our economy then, and many more that are not true now. Not for many years after I left college did I learn that the Greeks, far from being a detached and judicious people surrounded by chaste white temples, were hot-tempered, noisy, quarrelsome, and liked to cover their temples with gold leaf and bright paint; or that most of the citizens of Imperial Rome, far from living in houses in which the rooms surrounded an atrium, or central court, lived in multistory tenements, one of which was perhaps the largest building in the ancient world. The child who really remembered everything he heard in school would live his life believing many things that were not so.

Moreover, we cannot possibly judge what knowledge will be most needed forty, or twenty, or even ten years from now. At school, I studied Latin and French. Few of the teachers who claimed then that Latin was essential would make as strong a case for it now; and the French might better have been Spanish, or better yet, Russian. Today the schools are busy teaching Russian; but perhaps they should be teaching Chinese, or Hindi, or who-knows-what?

> When I wrote this, everyone would have laughed at the suggestion that we might be wise to start learning Japanese.

Besides physics, I studied chemistry, then perhaps the most popular of all science courses; but I would probably have done better to study biology, or ecology, if such a course had been offered (it wasn't). We always find out, too late, that we don't have the experts we need, that in the past we studied the wrong things; but this is bound to remain so. Since we can't know what knowledge will be most needed in the future, it is senseless to try to teach it in advance. Instead, we should try to turn out people who love learning so much and learn so well that they will be able to learn whatever needs to be learned.

How can we say, in any case, that one piece of

knowledge is more important than another, or indeed, what we really say, that some knowledge is essential and the rest, as far as school is concerned, worthless? A child who wants to learn something that the school can't and doesn't want to teach him will be told not to waste his time. But how can we say that what he wants to know is less important than what we want him to know? We must ask how much of the sum of human knowledge anyone can know at the end of his schooling. Perhaps a millionth. Are we then to believe that one of these millionths is so much more important than another? Or that our social and national problems will be solved if we can just figure out a way to turn children out of schools knowing two millionths of the total, instead of one? Our problems don't arise from the fact that we lack experts enough to tell us what needs to be done, but out of the fact that we do not and will not do what we know needs to be done now.

Learning is not everything, and certainly one piece of learning is as good as another. One of my brightest and boldest fifth-graders was deeply interested in snakes. He knew more about snakes than anyone I've ever known. The school did not offer herpetology; snakes were not in the curriculum; but as far as I was concerned, any time he spent learning about snakes was better spent than in ways I could think of to spend it; not least of all because, in the process of learning about snakes, he learned a great deal more about many other things than I was able to "teach" those unfortunates in my class who were not interested in anything at all. In another fifth-grade class, studying Romans in Britain, I saw a boy trying to read a science book behind the cover of his desk. He was spotted and made to put the book away and listen to the teacher; with a heavy sigh he did so. What was gained here? She traded a chance for an hour's real learning about science for, at best, an hour's temporary learning about history—much more probably no learning at all, just an hour's worth of daydreaming and resentful thoughts about school.

It is not subject matter that makes some learning more valuable than others, but the spirit in which the work is done. If a child is doing the kind of learning that most children do in school, when they learn at all—swallowing words, to spit back at the teacher on demand—he is wasting his time, or rather, we are wasting it for him. This learning will not be permanent, or relevant, or useful. But a child who is learning naturally, following his curiosity where it leads him, adding to his mental model of reality whatever he needs and can find a place for, and rejecting without fear or guilt what he does not need, is growing—in knowledge, in the love of learning, and in the ability to learn. He is on his way to becoming the kind of person we need in our society, and that our "best" schools and colleges are *not* turning out, the kind of person who, in Whitney Griswold's words, seeks and finds meaning, truth, and enjoyment in everything he does. All his life he will go on learning. Every experience will make his mental model of reality more complete and more true to life, and thus make him more able to deal realistically, imaginatively, and constructively with whatever new experience life throws his way.

We cannot have real learning in school if we think

it is our duty and our right to tell children what they must learn. We cannot know, at any moment, what particular bit of knowledge or understanding a child needs most, will most strengthen and best fit his model of reality. Only he can do this. He may not do it very well, but he can do it a hundred times better than we can. The most we can do is try to help, by letting him know roughly what is available and where he can look for it. Choosing what he wants to learn and what he does not is something he must do for himself.

There is one more reason, and the most important one, why we must reject the idea of school and classroom as places where, most of the time, children are doing what some adult tells them to do. The reason is that there is no way to coerce children without making them afraid, or more afraid. We must not try to fool ourselves into thinking that this is not so. The would-be progressives, who until recently had great influence over most American public school education, did not recognize this—and still do not. They thought, or at least talked and wrote as if they thought, that there were good ways and bad ways to coerce children (the bad ones mean, harsh, cruel, the good ones gentle, persuasive, subtle, kindly), and that if they avoided the bad and stuck to the good they would do no harm. This was one of their greatest mistakes, and the main reason why the revolution they hoped to accomplish never took hold.

The idea of painless, nonthreatening coercion is an illusion. Fear is the inseparable companion of coercion, and its inescapable consequence. If you think it your duty to make children do what you want, whether they will or not, then it follows inexorably that you must make them afraid of what will happen to them if they don't do what you want. You can do this in the old-fashioned way, openly and avowedly, with the threat of harsh words, infringement of liberty, or physical punishment. Or you can do it in the modern way, subtly, smoothly, quietly, by withholding the acceptance and approval which you and others have trained the children to depend on; or by making them feel that some retribution awaits them in the future, too vague to imagine but too implacable to escape. You can, as many skilled teachers do, learn to tap with a word, a gesture, a look, even a smile, the great reservoir of fear, shame, and guilt that today's children carry around inside them. Or you can simply let your own fears about what will happen to you if the children don't do what you want, reach out and infect them. Thus the children will feel, more and more that life is full of dangers from which only the goodwill of adults like you can protect them, and that this goodwill is perishable and must be earned anew each day.

The alternative—I can see no other—is to have schools and classrooms in which each child in his own way can satisfy his curiosity, develop his abilities and talents, pursue his interests, and from the adults and older children around him get a glimpse of the great variety and richness of life. In short, the school should be a great smörgåsbord of intellectual, artistic, creative, and athletic activities, from which each child could take whatever he wanted, and as much as he wanted, or as little. When Anna was in the sixth grade, the year after she was in my class, I mentioned this idea to her. After describing very sketchily how such a school might be run, and what the children might do, I said, "Tell me, what do you think of it? Do you think it would work? Do you think the kids would learn anything?" She said, with utmost conviction, "Oh yes, it would be wonderful!" She was silent for a minute or two, perhaps remembering her own generally unhappy schooling. Then she said thoughtfully, "You know, kids really like to learn; we just don't like being pushed around."

No, they don't; and we should be grateful for that. So let's stop pushing them around, and give them a chance.

Since I wrote this, I have stopped believing that "schools," however organized, are the proper, or only, or best places for this. As I wrote in *Instead of Education* and *Teach Your Own*, except in very rare circumstances the idea of special learning places where nothing but learning happens no longer seems to me to make any sense at all. The proper place and best place for children to learn whatever they need or want to know is the place where until very recently almost all children learned it—in the world itself, in the mainstream of adult life. If we put in every community, as we should (perhaps in former school buildings), resource and activity centers, citizens' clubs, full of spaces for many kinds of things to happen— libraries, music rooms, theaters, sports facilities, workshops, meeting rooms—these should be open to and used by young and old together. We made a terrible mistake when (with the best of intentions) we separated children from adults and learning from the rest of life, and one of our most urgent tasks is to take down the barriers we have put between them and let them come back together.

But let me leave the last word, as before, with one of the children. Anna had been kicked out of her previous school as a hopeless student and generally bad kid. Her parents were rich enough to hire the "best" experts in the Boston area to deal with her. Their verdict was that she had serious learning disabilities, to say nothing of profound emotional and psychological disturbances. From the first day in my class, she was one of the most delightful and rewarding children I have ever known—brave, energetic, enthusiastic, self-motivated, high-spirited, affectionate, imaginative, talented in many ways, and a natural leader—one of the two or three children who made that class the most rewarding I ever taught. And as I have written elsewhere, though she came to my class almost a nonreader, by the end of the year, and without any "teaching" from me, she was reading and enjoying large parts of *Moby-Dick*. She grew up to be as interesting and competent an adult as she had been a child; when I last heard of her, as the world measures success she had been a success in several different fields by the time she was thirty. She did not break or let others break her spirit, the better to fit into a dull and bad world; instead she made the world make room for her, and so in her own way made it to some degree a livelier and better one. To help all children do this should be our task—and our delight.

ABOUT THE AUTHOR

JOHN HOLT (1923–1985), writer, educator, lecturer, and amateur musician, wrote nine books, including *How Children Fail*, *How Children Learn*, and *Teach Your Own*. His work has been translated into fourteen languages. *How Children Fail* sold over a million copies in its first two editions. John Holt, for many years a leading figure in school reform, became increasingly interested in how children learn outside of school. He founded a magazine called *Growing Without Schooling* which continues to reflect his philosophy.

For information about or subscriptions to *Growing Without Schooling*, write Holt Associates, 2269 Massachusetts Avenue, Cambridge, MA 02140.